IN
PLACE
of FOLLY

by
NORMAN COUSINS

HARPER & BROTHERS, PUBLISHERS, NEW YORK

For My Brother Bob

Contents

IN
PLACE
of FOLLY

I. *Primer of Nuclear War*

A ONE-SENTENCE account of the human race has been written by Bertrand Russell:

HISTORY OF THE WORLD
An Epitome

"Since Adam and Eve ate the apple, man has never refrained from any folly of which he was capable. The End."

The folly now clearly within the reach of man is the decimation of the human species and, indeed, the rejection of many of those vital environmental conditions that make life on this planet possible.

The purpose of this book is to contend that the world and everything in it can still be made safe for man. He can be at peace; he can be free; he can grow. In place of folly there can be sanity and purpose.

Life is made possible by the most precarious balancing act in the universe. A small shift in the distance of the earth to the sun could cause the earth either to freeze over or to burn up. A small increase in the total amount of radiation on earth could result in an assault on the nature of man.

The internal economy of the human being operates

through an endless number of delicate balances. An alteration in the ratio inside the body of salt to water, of oxygen to carbon dioxide, of red blood cells to white could put an end to life. Cutting off the supply of oxygen to the head for a few consecutive minutes could damage the brain beyond repair.

The law of the vital fraction is the dominant law of life. Each person is the product of an incredible triumph over impossible odds. The odds against his being born were at least 500,000,000 to one. That is, out of 500,000,000 sperm cells available for fertilization only one achieved fusion. No two cells were alike. Each had the potential stamp of a complete and unique personality built into it. It would be theoretically possible for one man to double the earth's population, in terms of available sperm cells, in a single lifetime.

In addition to the vital and elusive fractions, man had to run a gamut represented by the hundreds of thousands of years it took life on earth to produce a species with intelligence, sensitivity, an awareness of beauty, a sense of wonder, and an ability to change its environment.

Human life is the rarest, most complex, and most precious of all the prizes in the universe. It is this prize that is now in the process of being diminished and rejected—by humans themselves. The humans are tampering with the vital fractions. They are rearranging the vital proportions in the soil. They are altering the radiation balance in the atmosphere. They are damaging their own germ cells, producing defective creatures and canceling out hundreds of thousands of years of evolving development.

Until now man could perform all sorts of assaults on himself; he could cheapen life, debase it, cripple it, and kill it. However, he could not get at his own germ plasm, locked securely in the inner being of each of his cells.

But now, through radiation, this last fortress of his physical integrity can be pierced. The radiation he himself is able to produce but is unable to control can violate his genetic substance by changing the structure of the human cell. If the radiation is sufficient the final barrier to a human mutation may be removed and the descent to the lower order of life may proceed.

Here we come to the most startling fact of all about our own time. The nature of the power available to modern man and its implications are hardly understood by the people in whose name it will be used and on whom it will have its effects.

These new threats have sprung up so suddenly that their thunderheads have hardly been observed. They raise the question whether the direction of men's thoughts, conditioned by centuries of local environmental habits, can be adjusted to the new total demands. Are forms of human organization, shaped in response to the evolving needs of the past, adequate for present and future? Will old methods for protecting life now become the fuse points for exploding it? Is the nation any longer the prime source of security and safety for its people? If not, what is? Why is it that the greater the nation's insistence on maintaining its traditional absolute sovereignty, the greater the threat to its own people—and, indeed, to all peoples?

It becomes necessary, then, for man to develop a survival perspective. He must think in a way he has never thought before—about his uniqueness, about his place in the universe, about the meaning and preciousness of life, about his values, about his relationship to other human beings, about the new institutions or mechanisms that are required to deal with random and pulverizing power, and about the rights of the next generation.

Such perspective requires almost total focus on the new

kinds of force now being accumulated and, in some cases, already being used. The range of force goes all the way from a bomb that has the destructive equivalent of 1,000 tons of TNT to a hydrogen bomb containing the equivalent of 20,000,000 tons or more.

The latter bomb, however, does not represent the zenith of nuclear power. There is no practical difficulty in the way of manufacturing a nuclear bomb with the equivalent of 100 million tons of TNT or 1,000 million.

Indeed, there is now no theoretical or practical limit to the destructive power of nuclear explosives except the motivations of the men who make them.

So far as is known, the largest bombs now being stockpiled are of a 20-megaton variety (equivalent to twenty million tons of TNT). Perhaps one reason for stopping at 20-megatons is that it is difficult to think of a destructive task that would require a larger bomb. Here, for example, are some of the destructive characteristics of the 20-megaton bomb:

It contains 1,000 times the destructive power of the bomb that destroyed Hiroshima, Japan, in 1945.

It contains more destructive power than a mountain of TNT four times the height of the Empire State Building.

It contains more destructive power than a caravan of 1,000,000 trucks, each carrying 20,000 pounds of TNT.

Thousands of megaton bombs have been manufactured by the United States and the Soviet Union and are primed for instant use. General John B. Medaris has stated that the amount of destructive nuclear power stockpiled in the American arsenal is more than enough to account for 20,000 pounds of TNT for every human being now alive.

A more personal figure is that for every American citizen there are 300,000 pounds of equivalent TNT destructive power instantly available against flesh, stone, and metal.

A one-megaton bomb releases enough heat to convert a billion pounds of water into steam.

The explosive power of the nuclear bomb does not exhaust its killing characteristics.

At Hiroshima, the explosion produced a firestorm. The air swept in from all sides upon the target area, whipping up the flames. As the heat rose, a vast canopy of smoke spread up and out. The result was a swirl of air, drawing in fresh air to excite and feed the fire. Even at the edge of the firestorm, winds of 40 miles an hour carried the blaze. The large number of frame houses added to the intensity of the firestorm.

A 10-megaton H-bomb (500 times more powerful than the Hiroshima A-bomb), if exploded 30 miles above Yonkers, New York, could produce a firestorm that would take in an area from the tip of Brooklyn to Bridgeport, Connecticut. A 20-megaton H-bomb, if exploded in the air midway between Akron and Cleveland, Ohio, could incinerate both cities.

The average underground shelter could not offer protection to human life in a nuclear firestorm. The ventilation system, drawing in air from the outside, would quickly convert the average shelter into a hot-air furnace, with air heated to temperatures as high as 1,000 degrees. The shelters would have to be sealed in from the outside and would require manufactured oxygen. The entire supply of oxygen manufactured in the United States in 1960 would not meet the needs of a city of 100,000 population in an underground shelter for more than two weeks.

The problem of underground shelters is further complicated by the need for depth protection against craters resulting from nuclear explosions. A 10-megaton bomb exploded close to the surface would produce a crater 2,500 feet across and 240 feet deep. The New York City subway system, often considered a prime shelter in case of an atomic attack, could offer no protection against such a burst. The business of constructing shelters 400 feet under the surface for large metropolitan populations would involve the most complicated engineering operation in history —even assuming that the problem of manufactured oxygen could be solved.

Brick and concrete buildings more than a few hundred feet from the center of the Hiroshima atomic explosion were not destroyed. In a one-megaton explosion, however, all brick structures would collapse within an area of 200 square miles. Private underground shelters would experience "fall-in"; that is, a building and all the objects inside it would fall into the shelter.

Flying objects constitute a special hazard during a nuclear explosion. In a 10-megaton burst, glass bullets from shattered windows would shoot through the air at high velocities over an area of 150 square miles.

Another new experience for man in an atomic blast would be "translation" or "displacement." These are the technical terms used to describe what happens when people are picked up by blast winds and are sent flying through the air over considerable distances. A megaton explosion would "translate" some people into dead and deadly flying objects over an area of hundreds of square miles.

So far we have been considering the effects of a single bomb. It is likely that a prime target would attract not one but several bombs, with a corresponding increase in the severity of firestorms, overlapping blast effects, and size of area affected.

A megaton attack on a city rules out the possibility of effective evacuation of a metropolitan area. Apart from the question of adequate warning time, the people of any sizable population center could not get away fast enough or far enough to escape danger. Indeed, being out in the open would actually add to the peril—even though people might have been able to travel twenty-five or even fifty miles from the heart of the city before the nuclear explosions occurred.

Scorching winds from a single 10-megaton bomb would deliver serious injury to people even on the outer fringes of a 2,000-square-mile area.

In the early years after Hiroshima, before the advent of both the hydrogen bomb and the ballistic missile, the defense of cities was tied to evacuation procedures. Today, any mass evacuation is ruled out. Evacuation depends on adequate warning time; this no longer exists. A nuclear-tipped missile can now cross a large ocean in fifteen minutes or less. Even if there were some way of ascertaining the precise moment a missile attack was launched, a signal to evacuate would find most of the people just emerging from the buildings at the moment of explosion.

Because of this, the emphasis on defense has shifted from evacuation to shelter possibilities. But the hydrogen bomb is to the shelter what the missile is to evacuation. The relative cheapness of manufacturing hydrogen bombs and their availability by the thousands virtually insures the fact that any attacker would deliver as many of them as were necessary to wreck any underground system.

Theoretically, it should be possible to construct underground caverns 1,000 feet below the surface, operating through manufactured oxygen with vast storage facilities for food. Here again, however, the shortness of warning time would prevent all but a comparative handful from taking cover. A grave moral problem arises in the case of those shelters where people who have been hit by radioactivity are still able to seek cover. Present civilian defense policy plans call for barring contaminated persons—by force, if necessary. Indeed, each shelter has a capacity quota. As soon as this quota is filled, people who try to get in would be refused admission—again, by force—whether they are contaminated or not.

Protection against radiation in a nuclear war, like protection against blast and firestorm, is made incredibly difficult because no one knows in advance what kind and how many nuclear explosives will be used in a given area.

If only one nuclear explosive (one megaton) were used against a large city, the average radiation exposure for individuals over an area of 200 square miles would be in the order of 450 rem during the first 48 hours. A rem stands for roentgen equivalent mammal; that is, an amount of radiation sufficient to destroy cell materials in man or produce a biological effect. A dosage of 450 rem in one day would produce extreme nausea. About half the people who are exposed to such a dosage die. A dosage of 600 rem would be fatal for all experiencing such an exposure.

A one-megaton bomb, to repeat, delivers an average dosage of 450 rem over 200 square miles. But a 10-megaton bomb delivers a dosage of 450 rem over 2,500 square miles. Closer to the center of the explosion the dosage runs up to 3,000 rem. If a dozen 10-megaton bombs were to be used in a linked bombing pattern, the fallout would be well in excess of an average of 600 rem over an area of 10,000 square miles or more. Similarly, patterned bombing by a dozen 20-megaton bombs would greatly extend the range of lethal fallout.

In any case, the prime difficulty in defending a civilian target against nuclear attack is that the extent of the attack is unknown in advance. Elaborate preparations to build shelters to withstand a certain megatonnage can be negated just by stepping up the number of bombs or their potency.

What about people who do not live in or near metropolitan centers or military installations? They would be unaffected by the fallout of heavy radioactive debris from remote surface explosions. But lightweight radioactive particles are pumped into the air and enter the stratosphere where they fall out with varying intensity around the earth. Many of the radioactive materials are short-lived. After only two days the intensity of most of the radioactive materials is only one-hundredth of what it was during the first hour. At the end of two weeks, the intensity is one-thousandth of what it was the first hour.

The danger of radiation, however, is not confined to this kind of fast-decay radioactive materials. Danger also comes from the long-life elements—strontium 90, cesium 137, carbon 14. After twenty-eight years, radioactive strontium still retains 50 per cent of its energy. The half-life of cesium 137 is thirty years; of carbon 14, more than 5,000 years. Other radioactive materials produced by nuclear explosions are yttrium 90, barium 137, cerium 144, praseodymium 144, and unfissioned uranium and plutonium. In addition, the explosion produces other dangerous isotopes, among them iodine, cobalt, and strontium 89.

The slow-decay radioactive elements have varying danger characteristics. Strontium 90, like air, water, and sunlight, becomes part of the life chain. When it settles on vegetation, it binds into the molecular structure. It is chemically similar to calcium and turns up wherever calcium has a function. The human bone-building process requires calcium. When vegetables or meat or water or milk containing strontium 90 are eaten, some of the strontium is eliminated naturally. The part that remains does damage. Since the body mistakes strontium for calcium, it is drawn into the bones and bloodstream; it bombards the surrounding areas with high-energy particles. Radiation of this sort can produce leukemia and bone cancer.

Exactly how much internal radiation from strontium 90

is required to produce malignancy is not known. This factor of uncertainty has been responsible for much of the debate over the dangers of fallout. Some scientists contend that *any* additional radiation beyond that absorbed through natural processes can be harmful and even dangerous. Other scientists contend that there is a threshold of danger and that so long as the amount of radiation exposure or absorption remains below this level, the risk is virtually negligible.

Even those who hold to the threshold theory are not all agreed on where the danger line should be drawn. One fact, however, is vital. Between 1954 and 1960, there have been continuing estimates concerning radiation tolerance by humans. The estimates have been made by various authoritative sources throughout the world, including the International Commission on Radiological Protection. The presiding fact emerging from all these studies and reports is that human tolerances are less than were formerly supposed. In the decade of the 1950's, estimates of general radiation safety levels have been reduced from 300 roentgens accumulated over a lifetime to 30 roentgens. Some estimates have been in the order of 10 roentgens.

With specific reference to contamination hazards from radioactive strontium, the International Commission on Radiological Protection has suggested that 33 strontium units in foodstuffs be considered as a reasonable level of safety. A strontium unit is equal to one micromicrocurie of strontium per gram of calcium. In any case, exposure levels are for doses averaged over a lifetime. Exceeding the limits for short periods of time may not be serious.

Bearing in mind that 33 strontium units in foodstuffs is considered a reasonable limit, this is what has happened to some American foodstuffs as the result of nuclear explosions that have taken place since the end of World War II (figures on foods tested in 1958 and 1959):

New Mexico cabbage	120 to 315 s.u. (strontium units)
One lettuce sample	970 s.u.
Peas	250 s.u.
Minnesota wheat	111 to 213 s.u. in 1958. One sample: 606 s.u.
St. Louis milk	reached a seasonal high of 37.3 s.u., April, 1959
New York milk	reached 27 s.u. in June, 1959
Atlanta milk	22.8 s.u., spring, 1959
Spokane milk	22.6 s.u., spring, 1959
Fargo, N.D. milk	over 30 s.u.
Moorehead, Minnesota milk	20.6 s.u.

There is no comparison with pre-1945 figures. Before Hiroshima and nuclear testing, no radioactive strontium existed in human bodies or food. Radioactive strontium exists nowhere in nature; it is man-made.

It should be emphasized that the U.S. Atomic Energy Commission did not accept the international standard prior to September, 1960. Until that date, AEC officials contended that 100 strontium units, and perhaps even double that amount, offered an ample margin of safety. The National Committee on Radiation Protection and Measurements, which was created for the purpose of evaluating radiation hazards, has suggested a "guideline" of 33 micromicrocuries per kilogram of diet.

Even according to fairly liberal safety estimates, however, it will be seen that some foodstuffs have approached or passed the danger line. Meanwhile, whatever the precise margin of safety may be, the undisputed fact is that every child in the United States now contains detectable traces of radioactive strontium in his bones. The same statement is probably also true of every child in the Northern Hemisphere, although studies have not been made in a number of countries.

It is also true that, as the result of nuclear testing, every quart of milk now contains measurable traces of radioactive strontium. Here are the figures from milk samples in the United States and Canada examined in 1958 and 1959. (The samples were examined by Consumers Union and were uncontested by the Atomic Energy Commission.)

CONCENTRATIONS OF STRONTIUM 90 IN MILK

Atlanta	7.9	Memphis	13.6
Austin	2.5	Miami	4.6
Bangor	7.1	Minneapolis	9.2
Birmingham	7.4	New Orleans	15.6
Bismarck	14.1	New York City	10.5
Boise	6.1	Norfolk	10.6
Boston	13.9	North Platte	9.4
Buffalo	6.6	Philadelphia	5.0
Casper	7.8	Phoenix	3.3
Charleston	7.3	Pittsburgh	13.7
Charlotte	9.5	Portland	6.6
Chicago	12.6	Quebec	13.6
Cleveland	8.8	Rapid City	11.2
Columbia	6.9	St. Louis	11.1
Denver	5.9	Salt Lake City	5.2
Des Moines	10.6	San Francisco	2.6
Duluth	11.5	Santa Fe	5.1
El Paso	3.3	Sault Ste. Marie	5.4
Great Falls	8.8	Seattle	10.1
Houston	4.4	Spokane	6.2
Indianapolis	7.6	Tulsa	8.7
Jackson	8.6	Washington, D.C.	9.8
Juneau	4.9	Wichita	8.1
Las Vegas	2.3	Winnipeg	9.5
Louisville	9.8		

The full significance of these figures is represented by the fact that strontium is collected and stored in the body.

Thus, a single glass or quart of milk has a low strontium unit count. But a child who drinks a quart of milk a day consumes 30 quarts a month; 360 a year; 3,600 in ten years. This doesn't mean that every unit of strontium ingested takes up residence in the bones; actually, only a small fraction of the strontium is stored in this fashion. However, increased exposure results in increased risk.

The bones of children require more calcium than the bones of adults. Therefore, the bones of children are more vulnerable to strontium 90 than the bones of adults. The increase in the rate of leukemia for children coming to maturity in the period following 1965 will be proportionate to the increase in total radioactive ingestion and exposure.

Fallout of radioactive strontium will not cease the moment nuclear testing is discontinued. Since the rate of decay is very slow, the burden in human bones will continue for many years. The average diet of an American adult by 1965 will run in excess of 50 strontium units, according to estimates. In parts of the world, notably Japan, the count may be higher.

So much for radioactive strontium. Next, consider cesium 137, another important radioactive hazard resulting from nuclear explosions.

Unlike strontium 90, cesium 137 has no safety limits. No "threshold" debate exists about radioactive cesium. It finds a home in human muscle. Its decay is somewhat slower than strontium 90 but most of it does not remain in the body for more than two or three weeks. It does not have the same opportunity as strontium 90 to bombard tissues and blood cells. This means its cancer-causing powers are sharply reduced. Cesium 137 poses a different primary danger. It emits gamma rays that are injurious to human genes. The principal sufferers will be future generations.

Like strontium 90, cesium 137 has its special characteristics. It causes the body to mistake it for potassium. Since milk contains potassium, children acquire cesium as a regular and continuing part of their diet.

Milk is not the only carrier of cesium 137. Here are some figures for food samples in the United States in which radioactive cesium has already turned up:

Dairy products	18.0 c.u.	(cesium units)
Meat	7.5 c.u.	
Flour and cereals	2.4 c.u.	
Citrus fruits	0.9 c.u.	
Vegetables	1.8 c.u.	

It has been estimated that by 1965 the average cesium level in human bodies will be 150 c.u.—even if no additional nuclear explosions take place.

What kind of genetic damage can be produced by cesium 137? Depending on the amount of radiation, cesium 137 can alter the characteristics passed on to children through germ plasm; it can produce stillbirths and malformations of various kinds; it can increase susceptibility to diseases; it can produce a general debility.

Most assuredly, it cannot improve the species.

Carbon 14 is similar to cesium 137 in its effects; that is, it represents a genetic hazard. While the danger to any given individual is extremely small, and while the number of malformations it may produce in our lifetime is almost infinitesimal, it has the slowest rate of decay of any of the radioactive elements. After 5,600 years carbon 14 still has half its original energy.

Not all the dangers of setting off even a few nuclear bombs were fully anticipated by the governments involved in the manufacture of these weapons.

In 1953, spokesmen for the U.S. Atomic Energy Commission saw no danger from testing to persons outside the testing zone. Little or nothing was said officially about strontium 90, cesium 137, and carbon 14. By 1956, however, the AEC acknowledged a negligible hazard. One year later, there was official recognition of a small risk. By 1958, AEC officials were referring to real dangers. In 1959, it was stated that there were specific limits to testing, beyond which nuclear explosions would constitute grave hazards.

One of the factors contributing to the public awareness is linked to an accident. The test explosion of a fission-fusion-fission bomb on March 1, 1954, resulted in lethal fallout far outside the prohibited zone. A Japanese fishing vessel, the *Lucky Dragon,* was exposed to a rain of hot radioactive ashes; many members of the crew became severely ill. Up to this point, nothing had been said publicly about the fission-fusion-fission bomb. But the announcement by Japanese authorities of the injuries suffered by the fishermen was accompanied by an analysis of the radioactive materials involved. Among these were uranium 237, indicating that the explosion had utilized neutrons not otherwise available in a simple fission explosion.

The first official U.S. reaction to the incident was that the *Lucky Dragon* had wandered into the prohibited area. This was incorrect. The *Lucky Dragon* had been hundreds of miles outside the testing zone. What had happened was that the fallout characteristics of the 3F bomb had not been foreseen.

Another serious incident resulting from the March 1, 1954, explosion took place in the Marshall Islands, an area that had been clearly designated as safe by the U.S. Atomic Energy Commission because of its distance from the nuclear testing site. A heavy radioactive shower fell on the Marshall Islands, producing a wave of radiation illnesses among the people.

Here, too, the Atomic Energy Commission did not take

the initiative in revealing either the fact of the accident or the extent of the injuries. Little by little, however, the matter came to light and was confirmed by authorities.

The U.S. is not the only nation to experience radiation accidents. On October 10, 1957, a reactor in Great Britain pumped some fission materials from its chimney. Particles of radioactive iodine, emitted from the stack, were deposited over the countryside. This was translated into milk contamination within a few days. Samples of milk showed twice as much radioactive iodine as was considered tolerable. The milk was immediately impounded in the affected area.

It is known that Yugoslavia experienced a severe accident in October, 1958. Six workers at an atomic energy installation near Belgrade were exposed to an uncontrolled fission reaction. One of the men died; the others suffered from extreme nausea, vomiting, and general debility but eventually made a substantial recovery. Nothing could be determined about the injury to their genes or any alteration in their life expectancy.

From the Soviet Union came unsubstantiated reports of at least one mammoth accident in which people far from the site of a large nuclear explosion in Siberia were subjected to dangerous radioactive fallout. It is believed that the accident followed along the same general lines as the March 1, 1954, American H-bomb explosion; that is, the shock fallout took place far outside the test area. There has been no way of verifying these reports.

In any event, as the result of the various accidents, the world's peoples have become uneasily aware of the dangers of nuclear explosives.

What is most significant, of course, is the fact that these dangers would be multiplied many thousands of times in a nuclear war. The quantities of strontium 90, cesium 137, carbon 14, and other radioactive materials in air, food, human bone, tissue, and germ plasm as the result of test-ing would be almost microscopic alongside the quantities released in a nuclear war between major powers.

For example, it has been estimated by some military ex-perts testifying before U.S. Congressional Committees that the first wave of an attack might involve some 3,000 nu-clear megatons—or the destructive equivalent of 6,000,-000,000,000 pounds of TNT. Successive attacks could bring the total above 10,000 megatons.

If the United States were hit by a large number of nu-clear bombs totaling 10,000 megatons, the blast, firestorms, and intense radiation would doom perhaps 90 to 95 per cent of the population centers—instantly or eventually.

For those not immediately affected by the explosions—that is, those in the outlying or farm areas—the chance for survival depends on the extent of radiation exposure. It has been estimated that a 10,000-megaton attack could kill 60 to 70 per cent of the people *outside* the population centers through high radiation.

An attack of 20,000 megatons could kill 95 per cent of the total population of the United States.

These figures are somewhat smaller for the Soviet Union because of the lower density of population and larger land mass.

Whatever the casualties in a nuclear war involving the United States and the Soviet Union, however, one prime fact must not be overlooked.

Millions of lives outside both countries would be claimed by the nuclear explosions. It will be impossible, in fact, for both major powers to smash each other without at the same time smashing a large portion of the world's population.

Uncontested estimates have placed the nuclear stockpile in the United States in excess of 25,000 megatons. General John B. Medaris' estimate of destructive power equivalent to 10 tons of TNT for every person now alive would translate into 25,000,000,000 tons of TNT. Dividing this by 1,000,000 tons (one megaton) gives 25,000 megatons. This would represent thousands of nuclear explosives, ranging all the way from small kiloton bombs (with an equivalent of at least 1,000 tons of TNT for each) to the large million-ton or megaton equivalent.

Assuming that the Soviet Union, which built a hydrogen bomb earlier than the United States, has at least the same available megatonnage, this would mean that both countries have a combined total of more than 50,000 megatons available for military use.

It is not necessary to take into account the nuclear explosives being stockpiled by Great Britain and France or any new nations that come into possession of nuclear weapons. Even if the United States and the Soviet Union employ only half their nuclear arsenals in another war, the damage to life outside both countries would be on a large scale.

The use of 25,000 megatons would come close to providing a saturation effect for the nations directly involved—through nuclear firestorm, blast, and fast-decay radiation. But the national boundary lines do not serve as retaining walls against radiation or scorching winds.

An attack on the United States in the order of 12,500 megatons would produce wholesale casualties throughout the North American continent.

An attack on the U.S.S.R. with 12,500 megatons would produce casualties throughout Europe, especially in the central portions.

The greatest danger to people outside the warring countries would come not from firestorm or blast or fast-decay radiation, but from slow-decay radioactive elements —strontium 90, cesium 137, carbon 14. The fallout would be world-wide, although the main burden, because of the prevailing winds, would rest on the peoples north of the equator.

Slow-decay radiation from the explosion of 25,000 megatons would probably have a permanent effect on most forms of life. (Nematodes and ants are said to enjoy natural resistance characteristics.) The larger quantities of cesium 137 could bring about breaks or fissures in the individual chromosome units, depending on the extent of the exposure.

This does not necessarily mean that all life will be de-

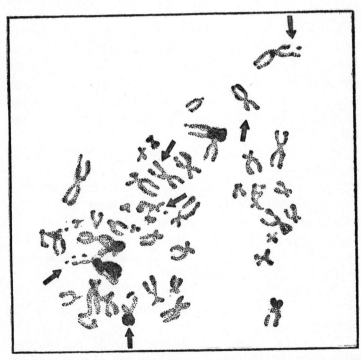

Chromosomes broken by irradiation with an X-ray dosage of 75 roentgens. Arrows show the breaks. Such breaks soon reseal themselves. (From T. T. Puck, in *Proceedings of the National Academy of Sciences,* August, 1958, pp. 772-780.)

formed or enfeebled after a nuclear war. What it means is that the conditions of life, certainly in the Northern Hemisphere, will be substantially altered. Most of the arable land and livestock will be contaminated in varying degrees. Open air and sunshine may cease being a joyous, cordial habitat and may be regarded as inimical and hostile to humankind. Any non-shielded experience is bound to be shunned.

The central question emerging from this problem, of course, is whether any nation, even in its own defense, has the right to tear down half the rest of the world and damage the prospects of all mankind.

II. *Special-Delivery Systems for War*

THE two greatest revolutions in scientific technology have come about at approximately the same time. One is represented by force; the other by speed. The two revolutions are wedded in the nuclear-tipped ballistic missile.

Missiles possess the same diversity as other families of weapons. Just as guns run all the way from the .22 calibre pistol to the 16-inch cannon, missiles come in different sizes and have different characteristics and purposes. Even the secondary power requirements for missiles vary from a few hundred watts to a thousand kilowatts. Some missiles are designed to be launched from mobile surface stations; some are launched from aircraft; some from stationary platforms; some from submarines and so forth.

In general, missiles are divided into what are technically known as "surface-to-surface," "surface-to-air," "air-to-surface," and "air-to-air." For nontechnical purposes, however, they are classified in this chapter according to range:

1. Short range, i.e., anything up to 200 miles. For example, the U.S. Marines have developed a 25-pound missile with a range of one mile and a speed of less than 200 miles per hour, for use against tanks. Also short range but devised for an entirely different purpose is a missile with a 200-mile range developed by the U.S. Air Force for use from

the ground against flying objects. It has a speed of some 2,000 miles per hour and can carry a nuclear warhead. In between are at least a dozen short-range missiles which have a multiplicity of purposes.

2. Intermediate-range missiles (IRBM); i.e., anything within a range of 200 miles to 1,500 miles. One example would be the U.S. Air Force "Hound Dog" nuclear-tipped missile, fired from jet planes against ground targets with a speed of 1,400 miles per hour and a range of 500 miles. (Technically, Hound Dog is known as a "cruise" missile.) The U.S. Navy has a missile ("Polaris") that can be fired from a submerged submarine and can carry an atomic explosive over a distance of 1,200 miles.

3. Long-range or intercontinental ballistic missiles (ICBM); i.e., anything with a range in excess of 1,500 miles. The U.S. Air Force "Thor" operates just above the medium-distance register. The Air Force "Atlas" and "Titan" can carry nuclear explosives over distances of 5,500 miles or more. All are operated from surface launching stations against surface targets.

Atomic or fission bombs can be fitted into the short-range and intermediate-range missiles, although some of the latter can carry hydrogen bombs. Intercontinental ballistic missiles are mechanically capable of carrying large hydrogen bombs. An error of a mile or more is considered standard operating procedure for an ICBM. A major factor dictating the use of H-bombs in ICBMs is the high cost of the missile. Hence they are aimed only at major targets and carry a maximum destructive payload.

In its early stages, the H-bomb was too bulky and heavy to be fitted into an ICBM or IRBM. The big break-through came with the development of a light-weight, highly compressed hydrogen bomb warhead.

The significance of this development is that it practically guarantees that any war involving intercontinental ballistic missiles will be fought with hydrogen bombs.

Speeds of missiles, especially the larger ones, run up to 15,000 miles per hour or more for part of the journey at least. By the time the missiles start their downward arc, the velocity reaches twenty times the speed of sound.

The reason for the variation in speed has to do with the propulsion mechanism of the missile. In the case of the ICBM, the early thrust comes from rocket motors that are hooked together. After one of the motors uses up its supply of fuel, it drops away from the missile. The reduction of weight enables the missile to generate higher speed from its second motor which drops away at the proper time in the manner of the first rocket. Because of the heavy demands of these rocket motors, fuel accounts for most of the weight in the ICBM. It takes only a few minutes after leaving its pad for an ICBM to burn up all its fuel. Freed of its burden of internal rockets and fuel supply, the payload part of the missile continues on its journey, reaching its top speed on the way down.

A long-range missile launched from the heart of Europe would be over the United States in about fifteen minutes. In terms of clock time, it would arrive 5¾ hours earlier than the time it left.

No weapon in history presents more difficulty to military defense than the missile. Generally, the top ascending speeds of defensive missiles are approximately fifteen times the speed of sound. Missiles in descent, however, are about 30 per cent faster than missiles in ascent. This by itself is not as serious from the viewpoint of defense as the problem of detection and response time.

Another complication is represented by the need to destroy an attacking missile before its gets too close to the earth. Even if a missile carrying a 10-megaton bomb were to be intercepted at a height of 150,000 feet above a target, it could produce firestorms on the ground below over an area of 5,000 square miles.

Even more difficult is the military problem of defending

against submarines carrying intermediate-range missiles. In fact, the missile-equipped submarine is far better adapted to surprise attack than most of the other long-range missile launching devices. Intermediate ballistic missiles can carry hydrogen bombs because of the new light-weight features. This means that an attacking submarine could be far off American coastal cities and still have destructive access to more than 70 per cent of the population.

Within a very short time—if, indeed, it has not occurred already—high-megaton hydrogen bombs will most certainly be fitted into satellites. This would mean that space vehicles or stations could dispatch H-bombs to ground targets in matter of a few minutes. The explosive missile will be in descent at twenty times the speed of sound or more, thus decreasing almost to the vanishing point the chance of interception.

Purely in terms of military strategy, the main problem posed by rockets and missile warfare is the danger of surprise attack. The premium of surprise attack offered by the new weapons is so great that some military experts have observed that it virtually dictates the need to hit first.

Surprise attack is as old as warfare itself. Indeed, numberless wars have begun with a sudden onslaught, though many of these wars were prolonged for many years. In the early Greek wars, for example, both the Athenian navy and Spartan army employed relatively heavy sudden thrusts. Even so, the struggles were long and protracted.

By and large, this remained the dominant pattern of warfare up through modern times. Now and then, of course, a major new development or invention would give the attacker a decisive advantage. In 1346, for example, some 10,000 English soldiers armed with long bows crushed three times as many Frenchmen in the Battle of Crécy. Similarly, the use of air blitzkrieg tactics by Germany in the early phase of World War II came close to achieving Adolf Hitler's objectives.

In any event, up through World War II, the military significance of surprise attack was measured primarily in terms of initial advantage. Today, however, surprise attack can be overwhelming and decisive. Moreover, it represents a new imperative in atomic warfare. Revolutionary as the previous advances in weaponry and tactics may have been in their own time, they cannot begin to compare in their surprise-attack significance with rockets and missiles. Once the missiles are launched, even a fantastically high rate of interception permits enough of the carriers to get through to accomplish a pulverizing result. If twenty missiles— medium-range and long-range—were to be directed at a metropolitan center such as New York, and if two-thirds were to be knocked out, the half dozen that got through could convert the city into a radioactive waste. Even if only one or two got through, the destruction would be total or close to it.

Stepping up the power of a thermo-nuclear weapon from one megaton to twenty megatons or even more is one of the simplest problems in the engineering of the bomb. Hence, an attacker who fears a high percentage of interceptions could increase the potency of the bombs or the number of missiles or both.

A parallel problem for the defender is represented by the hazard of shooting down attacking missiles over his own country. As mentioned earlier, if nuclear-tipped missiles were intercepted and exploded on their downward arc, the effects could be severely damaging. At 150,000 feet, the explosion of a ten-megaton bomb could set off large conflagrations on the earth below.

An even more fundamental difficulty, of course, has to do with the virtual annihilation of warning time.

The inevitable response to this danger has been to look beyond counter-weaponry for guarding against surprise attack. The main emphasis has shifted to the arena of national intentions. This means espionage, whether in the sky or on the ground. And it is at this point that the interaction between possible surprise attack and the counter-measures becomes both crowded and volatile. The very measures that one nation takes in its own self-interest to guard against attack might actually result in forcing the hand of the other nation. And yet, the nation that fears surprise attack cannot be expected to sit back and wait for it to happen.

This, then, is the dilemma of the large industrialized nation in the modern world. It fears aggression, yet finds itself pushed in the direction of aggressive acts of its own to try to cope with the threat. Rockets with nuclear-tipped warheads, therefore, tend to produce the military conditions that accelerate the danger of war, even though all other factors may work for peace.

A corollary is that the pressures to hit first grow in direct proportion to the speed and potency of the instruments of surprise devastation.

Nuclear-tipped missiles define not only the nature of a new war but tend to dictate the circumstances that lead to it. They create the new rules of the game; they impose a logic of their own and shape their makers and tenders.

The historic function of the military has been to protect a nation against foreseeable acts of hostility and to win in the event of war. This function, always difficult, is now complicated almost beyond comprehension by the nature and danger of surprise attack. Inexorably, perhaps inevitably, therefore, those who are entrusted with the safety of a nation find themselves taking measures that actually increase the risk of war—even though these measures are taken for defensive purposes.

Defensive measures, however, no longer fit the traditional definitions. At one time, defense was a literal matter; that is, the answer to the sword was the breast plate, just as a later answer to the anti-tank gun was thicker armor.

In modern warfare, however, response to a new form of

attack is not necessarily a specific defense but a superior form of attack. For example, in the 1950's, the Soviet Union tried to equate or surpass the tactical advantage of American jet bomber bases through the development of long-range submarines with launching platforms for rockets and missiles, thus bringing every major American city within nuclear range.

The Soviet also leapfrogged into first place in the race for intercontinental ballistic missiles. This resulted in the most important single advantage in the military competition between the two nations since the time when the United States held a temporary monopoly of atomic weapons.

The main American response to this advantage was not the development of anti-missile techniques but a vast acceleration of its own missile program designed at superiority in this field. To be sure, strenuous efforts went into defensive research, but the overwhelming preponderance, in terms of men and money, went into the race for missile supremacy and superiority of intelligence systems.

In the meantime, however, the existence of a missile gap produced a precarious uneasiness among American military planners. The grave concern over the Soviet advantage has led to various measures that in themselves incurred serious risks. One of these measures involved high-altitude flights over the Soviet Union for the purpose of acquiring military intelligence and for mapping Soviet military installations from which surprise attacks might be launched.

The result furnished a striking demonstration of the primacy of military necessity over political objectives in the modern world. In May, 1960, one of the American espionage planes was shot down far inside the Soviet Union. The incident occurred on the eve of what was to have been the most important conference of the leaders of the United States, the Soviet Union, France, and Great Britain since the end of World War II. One of the key matters to be discussed at the conference was the control of weapons adapted to surprise attack.

The actual conference, scheduled for Paris, never took place, even though all the participants actually met at the initial appointed time. The incident of the spy plane led to a confusion of explanations on one side and recriminations on the other. The conference disbanded.

Thus, the dynamics of nuclear military policy produced a political effect at the highest levels. The effect was to upset an attempt to control the dangers of a runaway nuclear arms race and surprise attack. Thus, even in the act of falling apart, the doomed conference furnished dramatic proof of the need that gave rise to its being called in the first place. And it supplied drastic warning that some means would have to be found to cut through the volatile fears of surprise attack, lest the very measures that a nation might take against nuclear war might help to bring it on.

For even if a nation had no intention of provoking a war, the stage would be set for incidents and accidents beyond its control. The manufacture of atomic weapons carries with it the most extensive safeguards, but there is still the possibility of an accidental explosion that might be mistaken for enemy attack. In addition, there is the hazard, however remote, that jet planes carrying armed thermonuclear weapons may be involved in an explosion. Though the nuclear bombs are carried in an unarmed condition, there are circumstances of national alert under which the bombs may be armed and which may lead to an accident.

Even more serious is the possibility that a pilot in a plane carrying an armed nuclear bomb, or a submarine commander, or military personnel in charge of a radar screen, or an officer acting out of the highest patriotic motives, could light the nuclear spark. Nuclear warfare, by its very nature, requires a certain diffusion of decision. Many hundreds of men have been assigned to key stations in the effort to guard against surprise attack. Any one of them, acting out of what he considers to be the noblest motives, might jeopardize the life of human society. While elaborate precautions have been taken against human error or human irresponsibility, they can hardly be termed foolproof in view of the large number of people involved.

In 1958, a member of the French Air Force, disgusted by what he considered to be the weakness of the French government in the Algerian situation, took it upon himself to drop his bombs on an Algerian village. (He made a mistake from the air and hit a Tunisian village instead.) Such an event is a rarity, to be sure; even so, it happened and there is no way of guaranteeing that it might not happen again in the case of a pilot carrying a thermo-nuclear explosive.

All these factors belong to the dynamics and imperatives of the nuclear situation. Far from imposing restraints, the horror of nuclear warfare accelerates the possibility of conflict.

Meanwhile, a new development—new in the sense that it has materialized since 1955—has increased further still the potentialities of surprise attack and preventive war. We refer to CBR.

III. *CBR and MAN*

THE danger of surprise attack in modern warfare is not confined to nuclear explosives delivered by missiles. Modern scientific war research has developed advanced techniques against civilian populations quite apart from nuclear weapons.

The new techniques are called CBR—chemical, biological, and radiological warfare.

These techniques are not to be confused with the poison gases used in World War I, any more than the hydrogen bomb is to be confused with the mortar shell. The new methods are infinitely more effective and far more adaptable to sudden, overwhelming attack than the primitive gases of 1914–1918.

CHEMICAL WARFARE

Chemicals have a much longer history in warfare than explosives. At least five hundred years before Christ, the Greeks were using fire-making chemicals against their enemies. Some historians contend that chemical incendiaries were used in Greece as early as 1200 B.C. The Romans maintained and extended the practice.

Poisoning of wells is a form of chemical and biological warfare as old as recorded history. In the fourteenth century, the Tartars in Crimea hurled the bodies of plague victims over the walls of Italian forts. Two centuries later, the Italians developed an artillery shell that could deliver disease to the enemy. In pre-Revolutionary America, according to some historians, European traders gave blankets infected with smallpox to Indians in order to impair their fighting strength.

In modern times, the precedent for using poison chemicals in warfare was established by France and Germany in World War I. Thereafter, all nations involved in the war, including the United States, used various kinds of poison gases. One of the most effective of these was phosgene, a choking gas. When a gas mask was developed that could protect against phosgene, Germany introduced a vomiting gas against which the mask was ineffective. When soldiers tore off their masks in order to vomit, they were exposed to the phosgene in the air. Another poison weapon that bypassed the mask was a mustard gas; it produced savage blisters.

Modern chemical warfare falls into two broad categories.

In the first category are chemicals that exercise their primary effects on the human system. For example, hydrogen cyanide, cyanogen chloride, and arsine have been developed into gases, liquids, and solids for use against human beings. When these agents get into the air and are breathed into the lungs, they pass into the bloodstream, where they interfere with the oxygen supply, thus injuring the central nervous system.

Lewisite is another chemical agent which, when used as a gas, can be highly dangerous to human tissue. It is rapidly absorbed through the skin. In sufficient quantities, it can cause blindness and interfere with the functioning of internal organs.

The most revolutionary development of all in the field of chemical warfare has the code name in the United States of "GB." It is a nerve gas. It is odorless and invisible. It is easy to disseminate. It can be packaged and delivered by short-range, medium-range, or long-range missiles. It can be spread over wide areas or used in limited situations as aerosol sprays. It can even be used in tiny dispensers of the kind that carry deodorizers.

GB, now being manufactured by the United States Army Chemical Corps, and, so far as is known, by other major powers, acts like a super-insecticide against human beings. Like DDT, its effect is widespread and almost instantaneous. Exposure to GB in gas form is lethal in a matter of seconds. A liquid droplet the size of a pencil dot on the skin will penetrate surface tissue and kill a man within ten to fifteen minutes. Respiration becomes erratic, followed by severe perspiration, vomiting, lack of bowel control, and convulsions.

GB derives its effectiveness by striking at one of the most mysterious and vital substances in the human body. For many centuries, doctors and scientists searched for the magic fluid or agent in the human body that enabled nerve signals to be transmitted to the muscles. The heart muscle, for example, receives an impulse that causes it to beat rhythmically. Finally, medical researchers discovered this vital substance and gave it the name of cholinesterase.

Nazi Germany, in experimenting with insecticides, discovered some organic phosphates that were antagonistic to cholinesterase in the human body. The Germans called it "GA." When GA came into contact with the human body, either as a gas or a liquid, it struck at cholinesterase. This made it impossible for the body to carry out the various functions that are independent of the conscious intelligence. Its cholinesterase attacked, the heart would go into rapid constriction and soon stop. In addition, all the other functions performed by the body without conscious instruction

—blood circulation, peristalsis, digestion, cell reproduction, utilization of oxygen, temperature control—would be blocked by the sudden impairment of cholinesterase.

At the end of World War II, the Soviet Union captured the German Tabun plant that manufactured GA and moved it to the U.S.S.R.

The United States Army, which came into possession of samples of GA at the end of the war, went on to develop its own nerve gas, the present GB. In a given concentration, GB is up to twenty times more potent than the original GA. Utilizing a combination of organic phosphorous fluorine compounds, GB can create casualties even before its presence is detected. It can be spread in the form of poison clouds over large areas. These clouds can be created by missile release.

American military officials testified before a Congressional Committee in June, 1959, that, in many respects, GB is more effective against civilian populations than nuclear explosions. It has the additional advantage, they pointed out, of leaving the industrial establishment intact. Moreover, there is no radiation hazard for occupying troops or officials.

Testimony before the Congressional Committee also brought out that shelters, no matter how deep, would offer inadequate protection against nerve gases.

In the words of Major General William M. Creasy, former Chief Chemical Officer of the U.S. Army:

"If we go around gearing up our civil defense with underground shelters, to protect against the atomic bomb, and, instead of having the atomic bomb, when the guided missile comes over, it has a chemical or biological warhead, instead of saving people, you are guaranteeing sure death or sure sickness or whatever effect the particular warhead is designed to produce. As you go underground, you must have ventilation, and as you put in ventilating fans and air conditioners, you simply guarantee . . . it will go down that particular intake you have conveniently arranged and hit your citizens."

The second broad category of chemical warfare is new, having been developed only since 1955. These are the psychochemicals.

Psychochemicals, unlike the blood gases and nerve gases, are not lethal except in large quantities. They also differ from the other chemicals in that they seek a temporary result. The main purpose of psychochemical warfare is to change the human personality and eliminate the will to resist or the capacity to think logically and purposefully. Psychochemicals can produce confusion, cowardice, extreme submissiveness, mental aberrations.

A parallel family of psychochemicals can produce temporary blindness or deafness, or general paralysis.

These various psychochemicals are being manufactured by the major nations. They are made out of various lysergic acid derivatives. Like the nerve gases, they are odorless and invisible and impossible to detect by ordinary means. Advanced forms have been created and successfully tested on human beings by the United States Army Chemical Corps, the leaders of which have advocated their use in war or situations involving the national security.

General Creasy testified before the Committee on Science and Astronautics of the House of Representatives on June 16, 1959, about the Army experiments. He reported that men exposed to the lysergic acid derivatives turned into cringing, confused, and fawning specimens. He also called attention to the fact that a cat in a cage with a mouse was given a minuscule injection of the psychochemical. The result was that the cat fled from the mouse as though in terror for its life. General Creasy stated that it would be possible to introduce such psychochemicals into a nation's water supply, affecting large populations. The drugs retain their potency even when diluted in many parts of water. Their nature is such that they withstand boiling.

Psychochemicals can be used with equal effectiveness either against military personnel or civilian populations. General Creasy suggested the possibility that an enemy, with thirty or thirty-five trucks operated by special agents, could circle all U.S. NIKE sites, spread the invisible and odorless gas, and convert all military personnel into non-functioning cowards. The same could also be done to government offices and places carrying out vital services. The purpose would be to paralyze the sources of decision and retaliation—as an immediate prelude to atomic attack.

The research objective in chemical warfare is exactly the opposite from that of medical drug research. In medical research, the aim is to produce therapeutic agents and minimize the undesirable side effects. In chemical warfare research, all emphasis is placed on finding the agent with the undesirable and uncontrollable characteristics.

BIOLOGICAL WARFARE

While disease and war have always gone together, the full possibilities of deliberate use of manufactured microorganisms against human life were not systematically explored until after the end of World War II.

The United States Department of Defense has been undertaking extensive research in germ warfare. In seeking funds from Congress, CBR officials have expressed confidence that bacteriological weapons can take their place alongside nerve gases as cheaper and more effective devices against human life than nuclear weapons.

The central aim in developing micro-organisms for war purposes is to produce a virulent strain that can overcome the usual degree of natural or acquired immunity by human beings. Other valued characteristics include high-infection potential, fast reproduction, and slow rate of natural decay. Research centers have also been attempting to create mutant strains that resist counteracting agents such as antibiotics.

In general, five categories of germs form the basis of war by micro-organisms:

1. *Viruses*. Epidemics that can be transmitted in war through the use of viruses include psittacosis, Russian spring-summer encephalitis, Venezuelan equine encephalitis, influenza, pleuropneumonia.

2. *Protozoa*. Amoebic dysentery and malaria are among the diseases in this category. However, protozoa are not so easy to grow or transmit as micro-organisms in other categories.

3. *Rickettsiae*. Transmittable diseases in this group include Q Fever, Rocky Mountain spotted fever, dengue fever, Rift Valley fever, typhus, p typhoid. Manufacture and transmission of these diseases in war are considered attainable and realistic.

4. *Bacteria*. Among the potent types useful in war are those that produce plague, cholera, smallpox, diphtheria, tularemia, anthrax, brucellosis.

5. *Fungi*. The principal use of fungi in war would be against fruits and vegetables. However, human beings are vulnerable to coccidioidomycosis or Joaquin Valley fever, transmittable through fungus.

Supplementing these living agents are the by-products or toxins created by the micro-organisms. Some of these toxins are highly poisonous. One of them produces botulism poisoning.

The use of bacteriological weapons need not be confined

to their direct effect on human beings. Indirectly, human beings can be attacked by transmitting disease to animals and plants, thus contaminating the food supply. A wide spectrum of anti-animal agents has been developed for that purpose. These viruses and bacteria can be made to produce hog cholera, Rift Valley fever, rinderpest, brucellosis, Newcastle disease, and East African swine fever, among others.

Biological agents that can be directed against crops include fungi, viruses, insects, and bacteria. The diseases they create include wheat rust, potato blight, and blast disease of rice.

LeRoy D. Fothergill, special adviser to the U.S. Army Biological Laboratory, took part in a symposium at the 137th national meeting of the American Chemical Society in Cleveland, Ohio, on April 6, 1960. Mr. Fothergill considered the techniques of spreading infection.

"The overt means of dissemination," he said, "is aerosol spray in a biological cloud that is invisible, odorless, and tasteless. It permeates most structures, searches out and infects all targets permeable or breathing. It establishes new foci of contagious disease in animals, insects, birds, and people, and contaminates hospitals, food supplies, water, milk, kitchens, restaurants, and warehouses. The infection of an entire continent by biological clouds is possible under proper meteorological conditions.

"Covert means of dissemination through saboteurs are almost endlessly imaginable and nearly as endlessly practical."

RADIOLOGICAL WARFARE

Nuclear explosions have three primary effects: blast, fire, and radiation. In the context of CBR warfare, however, radiological weapons specifically exploit the use of radiation against human beings. Therefore, radiological warfare involves the dissemination of radioactive isotopes—not only through bombs but through non-explosive means or techniques. As in the case of chemical and biological agents, radioactive isotopes can be laid down in a wide variety of ways.

There is no difficulty in producing radioactive materials outside a nuclear explosion. Controlled reactors can be made to yield whatever quantity may be desired.

Whenever a nuclear explosion seeks its principal effect through radiation rather than through blast or heat, it falls in the category of a radiological weapon. Thus, the inclusion of a layer of cobalt in a nuclear bomb could create a radiation hazard far beyond even that of strontium 90 or cesium 137. Radioactive cobalt can be produced in incredibly large quantities. If a saturating radioactive effect is sought over a large area, cobalt offers quick, effective results.

Latest research in radiological warfare is directed to the development of a neutron bomb. Its purpose would be to attack large industrial centers or cities, killing off the population but allowing the machinery and the buildings to remain intact.

Research has also been directed to the creation of tactical radiological weapons for use in limited war situations. By laying down a barrage of radioactive isotopes with fast-decay characteristics, it would be possible, for example, to keep enemy troops from using an important mountain pass for a certain period of time. The short life of the radioactive materials would enable an attacker to occupy the area at the end of that time without hazard. Other isotopes could be tailored to fit specific military requirements.

In any event, the nuclear arsenal of the United States and that of other nuclear powers contain a wide variety of nuclear weapons designed to meet a broad range of radiation requirements, all the way from a small effect in a limited area to a saturating radiological effect over a large area.

Moreover, radioactive isotopes can be selected according to the principal effect desired against human beings. The following chart indicates specific characteristics of radioactive materials in their effect on man:

Isotope	*Part of Body Affected*	*Half-Life in Years*
Cesium 137	Whole Body	30
Carbon 14	Whole Body	5,600
Calcium 45	Skeleton	
Strontium 89	"	0.1
Strontium 90	"	28
Yttrium 90 and 91	"	
Barium 140	"	
Lanthanum 140	"	
Uranium	"	100,000
Plutonium	"	24,000
Iodine (131, 132, 133, and 135)	Thyroid	
Manganese 56	Liver	
Cobalt 60	"	
Cerium 141 and 144	"	
Praesodymium 143 and 144	"	
Neodymium 147	"	

SOME POLICY QUESTIONS

Many people hold the view that CBR weapons are so horrible that no country would dare to use them. Even though various nations are manufacturing CBR weapons, it is felt that this is largely for the purpose of retaliatory warning. Supporting this view is the fact that poison gases were not employed in World War II, despite their widespread use in World War I.

This raises the general question of moral restraint in warfare, as well as the efficacy of treaties designed to eliminate inhumane methods of waging war.

In 1899, at The Hague, many nations, including France and Germany, signed a treaty banning the use of projectiles filled with poison gases.

In August, 1914, shortly after the outbreak of World War I, France used tear gas against German troops. France claimed that this gas was not lethal, being intended for harassment purposes, and therefore did not fall within The Hague Treaty. The next April, Germany employed lethal chlorine against the British and French. Six months later, the British retaliated with chlorine. Three months later, the Germans introduced the choking gas, phosgene. Shortly thereafter, the French introduced blood gases. The United States used phosgene in the closing months of the war.

After the end of World War I, public revulsion and moral indignation over the use of the poison gases resulted in an unsuccessful attempt at Washington in 1921 to prohibit all war gases. This treaty was blocked by France and did not go into effect. In 1925, however, a number of leading nations signed a treaty at Geneva under which both poison gas and bacteriological weapons were outlawed. Great Britain, France, and the U.S.S.R. were among the signing powers. Among those which did not sign were the United States and Japan. In 1943, President Franklin D. Roosevelt declared that, under no circumstances, would the United States be the first nation to use poison gas or other chemical weapons in war.

In World War II, all the contending nations had poison gases available but did not use them. Some measure of restraint was clearly involved. However, it is believed by some military observers that poison gas was relatively ineffective in comparison to the new forms of warfare.

World War I was a war of attrition; it stressed defensive

military operations. Artillery barrage and poison gas were readily adaptable to trench warfare and the protection of long lines of communication and supply.

World War II was far more comprehensive in its techniques and objectives. The bombing plane was the prime weapon. Correspondingly, civilian population became the prime target. TNT and incendiary bomb air raids on cities, sometimes involving a thousand or more planes, were the principal means by which the nations sought to impose their will upon one another. Doubtless, poison gases could have added to the misery suffered by civilians and soldiers, but it is not clear that the gain would have been sufficient to warrant their use.

In any event, the fact that poison gas was not tried has led to a fairly widespread belief that CBR weapons would be proscribed in any future conflict. Indeed, some people even hold the view that warring nations will not dare to use atomic bombs.

What, therefore, is the likelihood that these weapons will not figure in a major war?

The significant fact here is that the military leaders have already advanced the case for CBR. Certainly, there can be no doubt that nuclear weapons will be used in variety and profusion in another major war.

First, the main striking capability of a major military power in the modern world is based on nuclear explosive force. In the case of the United States, the separate strategies of the Air Force, Army, and Navy are tied to nuclear warfare. The relatively small size of the standing armies of the United States, Great Britain, and France has been justified in military terms by the existence of nuclear capability. The billions of dollars spent on missile research and development by the United States are designed to produce a special-delivery system for nuclear explosives. The United States would not have built its "Atlas" or "Polaris" long-range missiles, for example, if they had been intended to carry non-nuclear explosives.

Moreover, the testimony of U.S. military officials before budget committees of the Congress has made it abundantly clear that they feel there is no limitation on their ability either to plan for nuclear war or to fight one if major war should break out. The validity of this working assumption has not been challenged by the Congress or any other branch of government.

Quite the contrary. The United States has officially stated to the world that it is prepared to use nuclear weapons rather than give ground in situations affecting major national interests.

The U.S.S.R. has made similar declarations. Leading Soviet officials have announced their readiness to use nuclear power in any major conflict.

Great Britain and France, in internal discussions of military policy, have identified their nuclear explosive programs as their main claim to major status in the realpolitik of world national standing. There has been no talk of restraint in the use of these weapons if a major war should break out.

The overwhelming, significant difference between poison gas in World War I and nuclear power in the next war, if it should occur, is that poison gas was *one* of a wide variety of weapons in World War I, whereas nuclear power is absolutely central today in the strategy and tactics of the major nations in their military planning. If any doubt exists about the use of atomic explosives in the next war, the military leaders do not share it.

CBR warfare, however, especially as it concerns chemical and bacteriological weapons, may be in a somewhat different category. President Roosevelt's unilateral declaration against the first use of these weapons, as well as what would seem to be a public consensus, have in a sense created a moral position of restraint.

The existence of this restraint is decried by the U.S. military officials in their testimony before Congressional committees. They have called for Congressional and public recognition of the need to be free of any prohibitions on CBR.

In short, the American military have taken an official position in favor of the use of CBR weapons in event of another war.

Their argument is that nerve gases, psychochemicals, and disease germs represent the cheapest, most effective, and, in their own words, most humane form of warfare available in the modern world. Moreover, the great advantage they see in CBR is that it searches out and kills people without at the same time destroying the great cities and industrial establishments.

Essentially, therefore, the case for CBR warfare rests on a simple proposition: It is less reprehensible and fiendish than thermonuclear warfare.

Of this there can be no doubt. A hydrogen bomb can incinerate several millions of human beings at one time, deform and disfigure millions more, and make a shambles of man's edifices and homes. Nothing in the long story of human horror can compare with it.

But the fact that thermonuclear warfare is more calamitous than CBR warfare is not a moral argument in favor of chemical and biological weapons. It doesn't make plague bombs and poison gas a humane form of warfare. Nor does it justify thermonuclear warfare.

However, once the position is taken that it is proper to fight a war with nuclear weapons, the case against CBR collapses. What is important is to make a case against both. For nuclear weapons combine the worst features of chemical and biological warfare with the worst features of war by TNT. As stated earlier, nuclear bombs cause disease— leukemia, aplastic anemia, and other forms of cancer. They also leave an indelible stain on future generations through chromosome poisoning. Therefore, any argument against CBR warfare also applies to thermonuclear warfare and vice-versa.

The existence of nuclear and CBR weapons should produce not merely revulsion but a determination to mobilize all our energies against war. For if the war comes, the question will be academic whether a man is dying of encephalitis produced by a biological weapon or aplastic anemia produced by radiation. There would not be enough doctors to try to give treatment or even to diagnose. City hospitals, overcrowded already under peacetime conditions, would be able to address themselves to only a minute fraction of the need; that is, if they were operable at all.

Difficult though it may be to get accustomed to the idea, a new major war would not be like most previous wars in history—marked by ebb and flow, by ground fought for and held or relinquished, by people taking to shelters during a raid and coming out at the sign of an all-clear to go back to work or return to their homes.

A new war would be like putting a torch to a bird's nest.

Any debate over the relative horrors of thermonuclear war and CBR war is a painful commentary on the human situation in our time. The real question is not whether the hydrogen bomb is more or less ghastly than the nerve gas, but whether human beings, before it is too late, can prevent a war in which either or both may be used.

Modern warfare, whether it features hydrogen explosives or anti-cholinesterase agents, is directed against human life in the mass, and the conditions that make individual human life possible. The answer to such warfare is to be found not in debate over relative situations of horror but in the control of the weapons, and, even more fundamentally, in the control of war itself.

For the crisis of man in today's world is represented not

primarily by competing ideologies. It is represented by power without control. The competition between ideologies is real, but this competition has existed in various forms through most of history. Superimposed upon the present clash of ideologies is a new fact. This is the fact that man is in possession today of almost total power but his instruments of control over that power are unscientific and indeed primitive.

IV. *The Case for the Military*

THE men who fashion the big weapons and who will superintend their use in war are not demons, despite the fact that they may preside over the death of more people than any other military leaders in history.

These are not evil men, even though they possess the power that can convert an entire planet into a radioactive wasteland.

In saying this, we recognize that one of the great dangers confronting the world is that the men who have devised the new poison gases or the new explosives or who have been producing bacteriological weapons may not be content to see their work go forever unused. A man wants to justify his work and take pride in it and see it put to use. The most vigorous arguments in the United States for conducting nuclear tests have come from officials of the agency concerned with the manufacture of nuclear weapons. Similarly, the principal arguments in favor of authorizing poison gases and disease germs in war come from the men in charge of their production.

Yet even these grim realities do not make evil men out of the CBR contingent. These are not brutes bent on projecting their aggressive natures to the society of nations. These men exist inside a context—and the context is the fully sovereign national state. They feel they have been placed in a position where they are compelled to deal with existing conditions and the logic that seems to them to issue therefrom.

Their assignment is to assume that all political measures directed to securing peace may fail. They leave to the citizen and the statesman the business of devising and appraising the non-military approaches—although they themselves must proceed on an entirely different basis. In the context of their own responsibility, they feel bound by the imperatives laid down by the new technology.

Indeed, these men are compelled by their jobs to do exactly what they are doing. Their ideas and their imperatives are shaped by the arena around them. Their job is to function in a world of competitive national sovereignties. Their responsibility is to a national society. So long as the world is divided into sovereign national units, and so long as the units exist in a condition of anarchy, their actions will be dictated by the facts that surround them.

They find historical justification for the view that the only way a nation can be secure against aggression is by being strong enough to deter it or repel it. They point to numberless case studies of national disasters in which weakness invited attack. They argue that the only restraint against the aggressor has been the possession by the United States of the atomic bomb. Otherwise, they contend, military aggression against small nations and eventually the larger ones would have resulted in world conquest.

They oppose all measures that would place any limit on the fighting capacity of the United States. Especially do they resist any efforts looking toward curtailment or control of nuclear weapons. The issue of a ban on nuclear weapons is of particular concern to them not only because it may hamper the development of new atomic weapons but also because it could lead to other measures of control that might deprive the United States of the most vital part of its nuclear protective shield.

They are quick to emphasize any flaws or weaknesses in plans directed to a ban on nuclear testing in particular and on the manufacture of nuclear weapons in general.

First, with respect to a ban on testing, they contend that no foolproof system of enforcement is possible. Even if they accept the position that all nuclear bursts above the surface or in the upper atmosphere are detectable, they see no way of guarding any secret violations through underground tests. They admit that underground megaton explosives and even reasonably large kiloton explosives will create earth tremors that can be picked up on seismograph machines strategically located at inspection centers throughout the world. But they contend that small kiloton test explosions can probably be muffled in deep underground sites. And since the future of nuclear weapons development, as they see it, is in the direction of smaller nuclear tactical devices, they oppose a ban as being both unenforceable and inimical to the national interest.

It is felt, for example, that only nuclear testing can furnish the kinds of answers that are necessary for the development of kiloton explosives in the warheads of defensive missiles. The need for smaller, compressed machinery in which to house an atomic bomb that can be fitted into comparatively small missiles, calls for persistent experimentation. If all nuclear testing is to be banned, whether in the air or underground, then they fear a situation in which an enemy nation may already possess superiority with respect to nuclear missile versatility or may try to develop this superiority through secret violations.

As for agreements on reduction or elimination of nuclear stockpiles, the advocates of security through military power see no reasonable basis for enforcement. They point out that there is no way of taking an accurate census of all nuclear weapons in the arsenals of the nations. The ease with which bombs could be secretly stored in a large country, or even in a small one, would make it essential to rely on the good faith of all parties concerned. And it is the precise absence of such good faith that raises the question of security in the first place. They are willing to admit that a large number of bombs might be surrendered as part of an agreement, but they fear that this might actually be in the nature of a camouflage tactic, with thousands of bombs held in secret reserve.

On the question of radioactive fallout dangers, members of this group see no serious risk in a continuation of nuclear testing, even when conducted in the atmosphere. They acknowledge the fact that radioactive contamination may result in a small increase in deaths, but they feel this increase is so small alongside the size of the total population that it should be seen in proportion and perspective. They point out that 30,000 people lose their lives each year in highway accidents in the United States, yet there is no serious movement to abolish automobiles. Even if nuclear testing should produce the same number of casualties—in itself a dubious proposition—it would not be an exorbitant price to pay for the national security.

Proponents of this argument feel that this is not the only respect in which the United States should be prepared to run serious risks in furtherance of the national security.

They hold that nuclear explosives, ballistic missiles, and CBR weapons all belong to a war technology in which surprise attack is a specific and growing danger.

Hence it may be necessary, they contend, to take measures that might otherwise be considered provocative in the effort to guard against such surprise attack. They recognize that the dividing line between acts of espionage and acts of war may be difficult to define, but they feel that any question here must be resolved in favor of the national interest.

Moreover, they contend that the enemy has a war time-table of his own from which he cannot readily be taunted or budged.

In the political arena they similarly feel that the nation must be prepared to undertake and accept measures that might seem harsh or not consistent at all points with a democratic heritage. For example, the operation of military bases throughout the world might not conform to ideal principles of correct behavior. But this, too, is an unhappy but essential price that must be paid for maintaining an effective, strong posture, one that both prevents the spread of a hostile ideology and serves as a deterrent to surprise attack.

Finally, they accuse advocates of disarmament and world law of being less concerned with freedom than with peace. Indeed, they charge the peace group with a disposition to surrender in advance rather than to stake their lives in the cause of liberty. They point to specific individuals enjoying world prominence in the crusade for peace who have stated they would submit to tyrannical rule rather than see mankind exterminated in a nuclear war.

All these contentions—that is, the contention of those who favor nuclear testing and who oppose any limitations on the war-making abilities of the United States—cannot be dismissed as the irresponsible notions of malicious men. To repeat, they take the world as they find it; they know of no way to change the present context of world conflict; their rendezvous, as they see it, is not with destiny but with inevitability.

It becomes necessary, therefore, to meet their arguments —not with outrage or contempt, but with serious and deliberate purpose. One can disagree with these men without believing he is dealing with personified evil. The essential evil, of course, resides in the failure of people everywhere to think through the implications of a new age that has made the world a geographic unit without also making it a governed unit.

Most of what follows in this book is in the nature of a detailed response. Two arguments, however, require immediate reply.

The first is the statement that the only alternatives before the world are nuclear war or slavery. This is tantamount to saying that the only choices are suicide or surrender. There is nothing in history or human nature that says this is so. If enough people decide to arrange the affairs of the human commonwealth in such a way that it can become an ordered society, that decision by itself can create a vast new forward development in history.

If present conditions make war probable, our clear duty is to move heaven and earth to change those conditions while there is yet time. The chances for changing those conditions may be small and the difficulties and the complexities may be great; but this is the nature of the challenge to modern man, alongside which everything else recedes in significance.

The second and related argument is that, grim though nuclear war is, it may be the only means of preserving freedom.

The reply is that the fight for peace and freedom is indivisible. Freedom to wander around the radioactive rubble of a shattered civilization, freedom to reflect on the failure of civilized man, freedom to witness the changed and deformed nature of a human being—this is not the freedom that nourishes the human spirit or that justifies the legacy of those who died for liberty in history.

The issue of freedom *is* relevant in the great debate for peace.

But freedom in today's world does not depend primarily on our readiness or willingness to fight a nuclear war. It depends on the *kind of peace we believe in and work for.*

The wrong kind of peace could not only jeopardize freedom; it could convert the world into the largest prison history has ever known. The means are now at hand—directed force, mass communications, mass control—to impose a brutal feudalism on the whole of mankind.

This kind of peace could come about if peace is sought as an end in itself and not as the means of meeting the main needs of a human society suddenly thrust together inside a single arena.

How peace is built, and the uses to which it is put, will determine whether man will be free anywhere on earth.

The fact that a large part of the world is now not free, and the fact that much of the rest of it is threatened with a loss of freedom, do not mean that the cause of freedom is hopeless, or that there is no point in working for peace.

Freedom, like justice, depends on law. And law depends on the specific machinery that makes it possible—the orderly processes of responsible government.

The real issue, therefore, is how we go about creating a governed society as the basis for human freedom.

V. *Nuclear Testing*

FEW debates in living history have produced more confusion than the question of nuclear testing.

This confusion, as indicated earlier, is not primarily the result of disagreement among the experts over the basic facts. There is no quarrel over the basic facts. The confusion results from disagreement over the significance of the facts.

There is no disagreement about the fact that radioactive strontium, radioactive cesium, and radioactive iodine do not exist in nature. These radioactive materials are entirely man-made. Strontium 90, cesium 137, and iodine 131 are produced by nuclear explosions.

There is no disagreement about the fact that strontium 90 can produce bone cancers and leukemia in human beings.

There is no disagreement about the fact that cesium 137 can cause serious genetic damage.

There is no disagreement about the fact that iodine 131 can cause acute glandular disturbances.

There is no disagreement about the fact that, as the direct result of nuclear tests, detectable quantities of strontium 90 or cesium 137 or iodine 131 can now be found in virtually all foodstuffs. Among these foodstuffs, milk is considered of exceptional importance, both because it is a prime source of nourishment for children and because it serves as a collection center for poisonous radioactive strontium.

There is no disagreement about the fact that detectable traces of radioactive strontium, radioactive cesium, and radioactive iodine have found their way into the bodies of human beings all over the world, the extent of the contamination being somewhat higher in the Northern Hemisphere than in the Southern Hemisphere.

There is no disagreement about the fact that poisonous radioactive strontium locates itself in human bone, where it is stored; that poisonous radioactive cesium locates itself primarily in human muscle, and that poisonous radioactive iodine has an affinity for the thyroid gland.

There is no disagreement about the fact that the amount of radioactive materials in human bone and muscle has been increasing year by year. In the one year between 1958 and 1959, the deposition of strontium 90 and cesium 137 in human beings more than doubled.

There is no disagreement about the fact that, whatever the risks involved in nuclear testing before 1960, the spread of nuclear testing to other nations could result, in the words of a U.S. Congressional subcommittee studying the effects of fallout, in a "serious radiation hazard to world health."[1]

Where, then, does disagreement exist?

The disagreement has to do with the amount of radioactive poison that can be tolerated by the human body. Some experts contend that there is no clearly defined danger line, below which the human body can successfully cope with radiation, and that any amount of radiation, however small, can be harmful.

[1] *Fallout from Nuclear Weapons Tests.* U.S. Government Printing Office, 1957.

As opposed to this, experts of the United States Atomic Energy Commission have contended that the human system can sustain a specific burden of radioactive poisoning without serious effect. These experts define the danger line at about 70 strontium units. Some of the world's people, including Americans, have already reached 14 or 15 per cent of this "permissible" quota.

The experts who say that any increase in radiation is damaging to human tissue argue that it is impossible to define a maximum permissible dose. They agree that the amount of radiation from nuclear tests may so far only be a fraction of the background natural radiation to which human beings are regularly exposed; but they point out that natural background radiation is a cause of bone cancer and leukemia. Thus, even if nuclear testing has resulted in an increase of only 2 per cent in the world leukemia rate, this would translate itself into many thousands of deaths over a decade or so.

These experts have calculated that from 25,000 to 100,000 persons have died or will die of leukemia in the period from 1954 to 1978 as the direct result of nuclear weapons tests conducted before 1960. The variation in the estimates is a reflection of the lack of precise knowledge concerning the "threshold" factor.

In statistical terms, the percentage of increase yearly in the world death rate represented by these casualties is extremely low. In human terms, the number of people affected would represent the equivalent of a city the size of Fall River, Massachusetts, or Cedar Rapids, Iowa, or Stockton, California.

One reason for the public confusion over the risk involved in nuclear testing, therefore, is that one group of experts has been talking in statistical terms while the other has been talking in human terms. Each group has been accurate inside its own frame of reference. One-hundredth of 1 per cent is small enough as a figure to justify the adjective "infinitesimal." But one-hundredth of 1 per cent of the world's population comes to more than 250,000 people.

The statistical view is reassuring to the individual who wants to know what his own chances are of contracting bone cancer or leukemia as the result of nuclear testing. Assuming that further testing will be discontinued, the chance that any given individual would contract cancer as the result of past nuclear explosions is so small as to be virtually negligible. But even a negligible percentage, when projected to the entire human race, can turn into a substantial and ominous number of people.

Another source of public confusion is that one group of scientists may be talking about what has already happened, while a second group may be talking about a given set of circumstances projected into the future.

If the question concerns the number of cancers occurring in a single year from nuclear testing, the answer would be reassuring.

But if the question calls for a *projection* of what would happen over a twenty-five-year period, then the answer might be as alarming as before it was reassuring.

Such a projection would probably be divided into three parts. One part would try to consider what the casualties would be in the period from 1960 to 1985, assuming all nuclear tests had stopped by the end of 1960 and that the human race had to cope only with the radioactive materials that would retain their potency during the quarter-century.

The second part of the projection would try to consider what the casualties would be during the period from 1960 to 1985, assuming a continuation of nuclear testing at the same rate that took place before 1960.

The third part of the projection would try to consider what the casualties would be during the period from 1960 to 1985, assuming a dozen or more countries were able to develop their nuclear capabilities.

The range of scientific opinion, therefore, would run all the way from the optimistic view of those who cite figures based on the effects of fallout during a single year under conditions of limited testing to those who cite projected figures based on a continuation of testing in which many nations take part.

The first set of figures might show that for 1960 the casualties may not have been more than one thousand for the entire world.

The second set of figures might show that for the period ending in 1985 the casualties could reach 75,000 or 100,000.

The third set of figures might show that the casualties would run into the high millions.

All three sets of figures would be substantially correct. The confusion arises out of a lack of public understanding that some scientists may be referring to an existing danger, some about expected danger, and some about potential danger.

Another source of confusion is caused by the fact that some scientists have been talking about danger from *external* radiation while others have been talking about danger from *internal* radiation.

Human beings are constantly exposed to natural external radiation. The sun supplies it. Certain kinds of rock supply it. Some building materials supply it. People who live at high altitudes receive more of it than people at low altitudes. But this danger to any one individual is so small as to be considered negligible as a factor in determining where he should live.

X-ray is a form of man-made external radiation. It is

not merely a sharp light that illuminates interior objects. It is a stream of particles shooting through the body and hitting a sensitive plate where the relative densities of the pierced objects can be recorded. On its way from the emitting end of the machine to the receiving plate, the particles travel like tiny darts through the human tissue, tearing cells along the way.

When human cells damaged by radiation take on a rapid rate of growth they can become cancerous.

A study in England and Wales during the years 1953 to 1955 established a specific connection between X-ray examinations of the pelvic regions of pregnant women and probability that their children would develop cancer. It was shown that an average X-ray examination doubled the child's chances of contracting a malignant disease.

It is important to emphasize that this does not mean that every pregnant mother who is subjected to X-ray examination of the pelvis runs a high risk that her child will develop leukemia or other forms of cancer. The percentage risk is very low. Low though it may be, however, it is still twice as high as the *natural risk* would be for a child whose mother was free of X-ray examination during pregnancy.

In any event, the main point is that man-made external radiation is *potentially* harmful, and the magnitude of danger increases with the exposure. Yet *external* radiation, whether through X-rays or natural radiation, is not to be confused with *internal* radiation. The latter is far more serious.

In X-ray examinations, for example, the radiated particles don't stay in the body on their way from the machine to the plate. They may do damage along the way but at least they don't take up residence in the human system. The danger from radioactive elements such as strontium 90, cesium 137, and iodine 131 is that they linger behind, acting like miniature X-ray machines inside the body. They keep sending out energized particles, subjecting the surrounding cells to constant bombardment during the life of the radioactive materials. In the case of strontium 90 and cesium 137, the radioactive materials retain half their strength for more than a quarter of a century.

As mentioned several times earlier, radioactive strontium has a preference for human bone, radioactive cesium for human muscle, and radioactive iodine for the thyroid glands. Since virtually all foods now contain detectable traces of radioactive poisons in varying quantities, it is impossible to avoid bringing these materials into the human system. The resultant internal radiation is more dangerous than external radiation precisely because it is directed at specific targets inside the body.

It is at this point that the difference of opinion among experts becomes an important one. There is no argument about the ability of the radioactive materials, when taken into the body, to do damage to human tissue. The question that has not been resolved is: How much internal radiation is required to do discernible and specific damage? Exactly how much internal radiation will cause bone tumors and cancers or leukemia or genetic damage?

Whatever the precise answer, some facts are clear.

First, human beings did not have poisonous strontium or cesium or iodine in their bones or glands or muscles before the age of nuclear explosions. This is a new hazard in human history, completely man-made and, so far, extremely difficult to counteract.

Second, whether or not a danger line exists, the amount of the poisonous radioactive materials in human bone and tissue has been increasing. In many places in the world, the level of radioactive materials inside human beings has doubled and re-doubled from 1955 to 1960.

Third, whatever the tolerance limits may be in human beings, these limits will definitely be exceeded if other nations test nuclear weapons at the per nation rate of testing established by the United States and the Soviet Union from 1953 through 1958.

Fourth, all peoples are affected by the explosion of nuclear weapons, and not merely the people of the country conducting such experiments. There is no known way of confining the fallout to the nation setting off the bombs, nor is there any known way of cleansing the sky of radioactive garbage.

Of these points, the fourth is by far the most important. The United States, the Soviet Union, Great Britain, and France have arrogated to themselves the right to contaminate the air that belongs to other peoples. Permission from those affected has not been sought. Representation has not been offered in the national assemblies of the testing countries to people whose crops were dusted with radioactive materials, whose cows have grazed on lands carrying a radioactive burden, whose children have drunk milk containing strontium 90 and cesium 137, whose leukemia rate has increased with the increase of radioactive materials in the air, and whose future carries a question mark to which no one has a precise answer.

It is irrelevant to reply that the actual damage to crops and human tissue is relatively small. Only the peoples affected have the right to determine whether they are willing to sustain radioactive contamination, however small or great. To a mother who has lost a child, the universe itself has suddenly become a void. The child is not a statistic. To the people of a country who learn that they now belong to the first generation of men in human history to carry radioactive strontium in their bones, the stark indifference of the testing nations is incomprehensible and outrageous.

In any event, issues such as these have created an increasingly powerful world public opinion against nuclear testing. This public opinion has been reflected in the over-whelming vote in the United Nations against continued testing and in opinion surveys.

Many advocates of continued nuclear testing have taken such public opinion into account. Indeed, they regard the hazards of testing as a strong argument in support of the case for underground explosions.

It is undoubtedly true that underground testing could be made to seal in the radioactive garbage. It is not yet known, however, how much underground shock can be absorbed by the earth without creating a compensating force, such as earth tremors or earthquakes. While the initial experiences at setting off nuclear explosions in large caves have produced no alarming indications in this direction, most of the underground explosions so far have been in the kiloton range; that is, in the order of thousands of tons of TNT equivalent. If the underground tests should get into the megaton range; that is, the equivalent of a million tons or more of TNT equivalent, there may be a valid question concerning shock effects. This is one area of human knowledge where even theory is shadowy. Man knows very little about the possible functions of the various substances and layers within the earth, or the relationship of shock in one area to eruption in another. Nor has the problem of possible widespread contamination of the under-ground water table been adequately studied.

Even should it be proved that underground testing carries no shock or radioactive hazard, there is no assurance that all the countries entering the nuclear group would feel obligated to do their testing in caves. When France initiated its nuclear explosions in 1960, it followed the lead of the United States, the Soviet Union, and Great Britain in conducting its tests in the atmosphere. Underground tests are many times more expensive than atmospheric bursts. They require vast preparations. Each new nation entering the nuclear arena may feel it should be entitled to the same favorable procedures used by its predecessors.

In the absence, therefore, of effective world control over nuclear weapons—of which an enforceable ban on testing is a vital part—there is no way to guard against an increase in general radioactive contamination of the atmosphere.

The counter-argument here is that to use the word "effective" in connection with control of nuclear testing is a contradiction in terms. It is pointed out that it is virtually impossible to guard against secret violations. A nation bent on developing new refinements in its nuclear arsenal could carry out its tests deep in the earth or high in the sky with very small probability of detection. The larger the cavity in the earth, the smaller the shock waves that would turn up on seismograph machines operated at inspection stations. At the opposite end, nuclear explosions conducted thirty miles or more above the earth—or even in outer space, for that matter—sharply reduce the chances of detection.

These facts are impressive but they do not destroy the case for a workable ban on nuclear tests.

First, even the largest earth cavities could not muffle the shock waves from a thermonuclear bomb with a destructive force measured in megatons. If a nation is attempting to avoid detection, it will find itself forced to confine its testing to the baby atomic bombs—which is to say, an approximate range that might run from 1/100 to 1/20,000 of the destructive power of the megaton nuclear bombs already tested.

Second, the probability of success in secret underground tests is cut sharply by the number of inspecting seismograph stations. As an example: If a world detection system were established, and if ten inspection stations with earth-shock-recording devices were maintained in a large country, its instruments might be able to pick up underground explosions caused by bombs with a power rating of fifteen or more kilotons. If the number of stations were increased to fifty, and properly located, explosions of ten-kiloton bombs might be detected. If the number of stations were increased to two hundred, the underground bombs might have to be under five kilotons.

In short, any attempt at secrecy calls for small bombs. The more powerful the bomb, the greater the risk of detection. And the more numerous the number of inspecting stations, the smaller the chance of successful violation.

The problem, therefore, is less technical than political. Even a one-kiloton bomb, when exploded underground, can be detected if enough detecting stations are properly installed and manned.

Third, while it is theoretically true that an underground explosion might be difficult to detect, the preparations for such an explosion might be difficult to conceal. A nation seeking to muffle the shock of a 10-megaton bomb in a secret underground test, would have to dig a hole large enough to take in the area of Rockefeller Center, in New York City, plus several football fields. The mammoth size of the cave would call for an earth removal operation comparable to that of the entire Panama Canal.

Advocates of a ban on nuclear testing are not therefore persuaded by the argument that secret violations are theoretically possible. They feel that the risk of secret violation is small alongside the risk of no agreement, no control, and unlimited nuclear testing. For, even if a nation should be able secretly to develop a small atomic weapon with valuable new features, this does not constitute as much of a danger as having a dozen or more others develop their nuclear capacity.

All the foregoing sets the stage for one presiding fact: The case against nuclear testing and for control of nuclear weapons does not rest solely on the danger of radiation or genetic damage to human beings, but on the increased risk of war it represents.

Testing by a few nations leads to testing by many. With each additional nation coming into possession of nuclear weapons, the difficulty of preventing outbreak of nuclear war becomes that much greater. Even if there were no problems in radioactivity, the spread throughout the world of this kind of power would gravely retard the chances for peace. Small conflicts become big ones the moment nuclear explosives are used. Large nations are intertwined with the smaller ones, whether with respect to spheres of influence, military bases, national interests, or political commitments.

As it is, the production of nuclear weapons by only a few nations has created an atmosphere of dreadful insecurity. If a dozen or more nations, large and small, were to possess nuclear stockpiles and the means of delivering them, the resultant uncertainty would produce fever blisters in the community of nations.

The dominant position of the large nations will be sharply reduced by the nuclear capabilities of small nations. Once a nation—large or small—fashions the means for manufacturing a fission-fusion-fission bomb, it can create a stockpile literally large enough to destroy the world.

The economics of nuclear warfare are congenial to the small nation. Nuclear power offers the cheapest method for producing death since the early Greek wars. In the war between Sparta and Athens during the fifth century B.C., the cost of killing a single man has been roughly estimated at $50. During the Roman wars the price of a single death is said to have approximated $100. By the time of the American War for Independence, the cost had climbed to $600.

During the American War Between the States, the figure was more than $5000. The estimated cost for killing one man in World War I was about $26,000; for World War II it was $65,000.

In a nuclear war it may cost no more to kill a man than it did two thousand years ago. Indeed, it is possible that the hydrogen bomb is the least expensive form of mass death to be invented by the human mind. A hydrogen bomb with the power of twenty million tons of TNT costs no more than $250,000. If TNT had been used, the cost would be in excess of $10,000,000,000. The reason for the cheapness of nuclear bombs is related to the high explosive power per dollar of investment. Increasing the destructive power from a 10-megaton bomb to a 20-megaton bomb does not double the cost of the bomb. Similarly, a 20-megaton bomb does not cost 1,000 times more than a 10-kiloton bomb.

A ban on nuclear testing, especially if undertaken under the auspices of the United Nations, with machinery for verification and enforcement, represents the best chance of keeping nuclear weapons from becoming standard items in the arsenals of the world's nations.

This by itself will not dispose of the threat of nuclear war. Even if nuclear weapons are possessed by only four or five major nations, this is a massive problem. But the fact that the problem is already incredibly difficult is no warrant for making it impossible.

Moreover, the specific exercise of authority by the United Nations in a vital matter such as nuclear testing could serve as an important proving ground for a stronger U.N. By holding the line against further testing, the U.N. may create the agencies which, if enlarged, could get into even more essential areas of nuclear control. It may be able to create and operate the machinery which could enforce a ban on the actual manufacture of nuclear weapons.

This brings us to the problem of secret violations, especially in the field of nuclear weapons testing.

It would require an extremely large number of inspecting stations—as many as a hundred or more—to monitor a large nation like the Soviet Union or the United States in a way that could detect such violations. But this task is well within the competence and reach of a world organization.

It is to be expected that some of the nuclear nations will resist the idea that they must give hospitality to a large number of inspecting stations, fully manned, inside their own countries. Accordingly, direct negotiations among the nuclear powers may not produce the substantial kind of inspection machinery that is required to do the job. Some of the nations may not agree to comprehensive, on-site inspection unless they feel absolutely compelled to do so. And direct negotiations provide ample opportunity to withstand such compulsions.

However, when the source of authority happens to be a strengthened United Nations, it may be difficult for any one nation to insist on a smaller number of inspecting stations than are essential to the common security.

The violation of treaties by nation against nation has ample precedent. But the obligations of a nation to a world society under law are something else, especially when individuals can be held accountable.

There is another aspect of nuclear testing that dictates the involvement of the United Nations. This has to do with control over nuclear stockpiles. Here, the United Nations would be up against the unquestioned fact that the large nations have secretly stored their nuclear explosives.

Obviously, not until the United Nations becomes a government itself, with lines of authority extending to the individual in those matters concerned with the common security of the world's peoples, will it be possible for the U.N. to enforce a ban on stockpiles. For only a governed world, with access to individual violators, will possess the functioning machinery to undertake a census of stored nuclear weapons and then bring them under control. Indeed, the existence of secret nuclear stockpiles constitutes a powerful argument for a world government through the United Nations.

VI. *Power Without Control*

THE crisis of power without control did not come upon the world overnight. It has developed steadily and inexorably since the day the bomb was dropped on Hiroshima.

Certain assumptions were woven into U.S. policy at the end of World War II. The biggest and perhaps most precarious of these assumptions was that time was on America's side, that security and stability would increase with each passing day, and that the world would gradually evolve into a settled international society. The U.S. had the bomb—a monopoly, or so we thought—and the fact of this power would give the world its greatest assurance of stability.

Fortified by these facts, the gradualists looked ahead to a long period of peace. Indeed, at San Francisco in 1945, the claim of victory was made largely in the name of gradualism and reason over the juggernaut of the irrational.

From that magnificent perch in 1945, gradualism and reason have slipped a long way. What has happened to bring about such a costly fall from grace and power? It is too easy to say that reason went on the defensive just because Soviet policy went on the offensive. Too easy, because it doesn't explain why reason didn't itself go on the offensive in what was largely a war of ideas. Nor does it explain why reasonable men—by which we mean those who spoke for the democracies—failed to take full advantage of the opportunity for world leadership that was theirs for the asking.

The failure of reasonable men since the end of the war consists of this: that they were unable or unwilling to carry over into the making of the peace the same boldness, the same daring and dynamism, that won the war and that was no less needed to win the peace. All the sterile clichés that are part of the ritual of apparent reason were used to sanctify the timid and inadequate approach to the making of the new world. The big need was to invest the United Nations with definite powers of government comprehensive enough to deal with the threats to the peace. If such a proposal had been made and then blocked by any single nation, then at least the proponents might have been able from the start to place the objector on the defensive in the battle of ideas. But the U.S. held back, intoning the pretty phrases of reason to the detriment of the cause of reason. "The world is not yet ready for government." "The American people are not ready." "No other nation would accept." "It's far-fetched." "Let's wait twenty-five or fifty years." "Time will work for us." "Progress is possible only through gradualism." "Let's not be drastic." "The present tensions, given enough time, will dissolve."

But there is no cosmic hocus-pocus that dictates that time will always serve the cause of reason. Time by itself is supremely indifferent to the petty and major problems that beset the human race. If the circumstances favor progress, time favors progress. If the circumstances favor disintegration, time favors disintegration. The job of the truly reasonable man is to create and enlarge those conditions which make progress possible, and to arrest or change those conditions which make disintegration inevitable.

The disintegration since 1945 has not taken place in a vacuum. The conditions were such as to intensify the crisis rather than to solve it. The world had become a single potential battlefield. Two nations of approximately equal power, with deep underlying fear and suspicion of each other, emerged from the war convinced that a war between them at some point was probable. The issues between them were deep and real, but not nearly so deep or real as the larger issue confronting humanity itself. That larger issue was whether this planet could remain safe for human habitation, and, if so, whether democratic values could be preserved.

In sum, the problem for the reasonable man was not how to win a new war but how to avert it—with honor and without knuckling under. It was a difficult problem—perhaps the most difficult one that has ever confronted men of reason in history, but the difficulty was dwarfed by the danger. And yet, critical though the problem was, there were vast resources at the call of the West. It enjoyed preponderance. It was in a strategic position to keep the initial tensions from getting out of hand by proposing the creation of an organization of the United Nations strong enough to guarantee security for the large states and thus deprive any state, large or small, of either the excuse or the opportunity to seek security through expansion.

But men of reason proposed and committed themselves to weakness. They justified this approach on the grounds that each passing year would find an almost automatic improvement in world health. They overlooked the fact that the principal danger of a weak organization was not so much that it would be unable to deal with crisis situations, as that this very weakness would actually create crisis situations.

Time has not been on the side of gradualists and reasonable men since 1945. Each passing day brought the world closer to the day when many nations, working entirely on their own and without benefit of the much-vaunted "secrets," would have their own atomic weapons.

And an armaments race is an armaments race, whether

with respect to atomic weapons, battleships, bullets, or bows-and-arrows. As the stockpiles of weapons mount, so do the provocations and the tensions—curiously though not surprisingly. And the final provocation almost magically coincides with the discovery by any one nation or coalition of nations that it has a decisive margin in armaments over the others.

But the American people had pennies over their eyes in the early years following the end of the war—pennies that prevented them from recognizing issues that would determine whether any of them would be alive twenty years later. These pennies were the domestic squabbles that became not only a national preoccupation but a national obsession.

There was to be no perceptible resistance to the idea of relying upon an atomic armaments race for security. It may be that the job of world control over atomic weapons and all other weapons of mass destruction was too demanding for a nation that felt entitled to a respite after a war. It may be that the American people were so fascinated with limited objectives and with ingrained ideas of gradualism that they could not understand the crucial need for a majestic awareness of the immediateness of the problem and a determination to come to grips with the seemingly impossible.

If this drift seems like madness, consider how the madness was multiplied in view of the new implications of atomic warfare. A bigger stockpile of bombs offered little or no security to a nation which was hit first, particularly since the first blow might be the conclusive blow. World War II may well have been the last war in which it would be possible to retaliate after the first blow was struck. For a nation which, by its very nature as well as by its constitutional processes, would not indulge in blitzkrieg aggression, a superior stockpile of atomic bombs might actually represent an added margin of danger in that it would increase the chances of that nation being hit first in order to get it out of the way.

If Americans ask themselves how it was that only a short time after victory the crisis was as serious as it had been at any time during the war, they naturally look back to see where the faulty turn was taken.

There can be little question that the first error may have been the biggest error. The first error was the atomic bombing of Hiroshima. Not the making of the atomic bomb; that we were forced to do out of sheer military necessity, for the enemy was working on atomic weapons as well. It was what we did with the atomic bomb after we made it that was a mountainous blunder.

In order to create a proper perspective, consider the report turned in to the War Department on June 11, 1945—one month before the New Mexico test, two months before Hiroshima. The report was made by a Committee on Social and Political Implications consisting of three physicists, three chemists, and one biologist under the chairmanship of Professor James Frank, of the University of Chicago. This report, not made public by the War Department at the time, is one of the most important American documents of recent years—even though it was virtually unknown to the American people. It was, in effect, a declaration of conscience and responsibility by scientists—a declaration that their first duty was to the general welfare, that they did not propose to stand aside in parched detachment while the products of their research were applied.

"In the past," they wrote, "scientists could disclaim direct responsibility for the use to which mankind had put their disinterested discoveries. We now feel compelled to take a more active stand because the success which we have achieved in the development of nuclear power is fraught with infinitely greater dangers than were all the inventions of the past. All of us, familiar with the present state of nucleonics, live with the vision before our eyes of sudden destruction visited on our own country, of a Pearl Harbor disaster repeated a thousand-fold magnification in every one of our major cities."

Soberly, and with great simplicity, they went on to show why no defense could be devised to offer *adequate* protection against a surprise atomic attack, and why only *adequate* international political organization of the world could offer any hope of security. They demonstrated why there were actually no "secrets" that other nations could not develop for themselves, working with the actual knowledge of nucleonics existing in scientific laboratories throughout the world, and that all we had was a head start of perhaps a few short years.

They explained the peculiar vulnerability of America to atomic attack; why its densely populated metropolitan districts and our concentrated industries could be destroyed by instant and synchronized sabotage, if not by overhead attack. They explained why a quantitative advantage in atomic bombs was only an illusory advantage. "We are in a less favorable position than nations which are either now more diffusely populated and whose industries are more scattered, or whose governments have unlimited power over the movement of population and the location of industrial plants. . . . Russia and China are the only great nations at present which could survive a nuclear attack."

Because of all this, the report said, it was of critical importance that the bomb not be introduced in a way that would jeopardize America's long-range security, however great the apparent short-range advantages. A surprise attack by us with this new weapon—without any advance demonstration and without any ultimatum—involved much more than local military considerations. It required a political decision on the highest level.

"Russia, and even allied countries which bear less mistrust of our ways and intentions, as well as neutral countries, may be deeply shocked by this step. It may be very difficult to persuade the world that a nation which was capable of secretly preparing and suddenly releasing a new weapon, as indiscriminate as the rocket bomb and a thousand times more destructive, is to be trusted later in any proclaimed desire of having such weapons abolished by international agreement. . . . It is not at all certain that American public opinion, if it could be enlightened as to the effect of atomic explosives, would approve of our own country being the first to introduce such an indiscriminate method of wholesale destruction of civilian life.

"Thus . . . the military advantages and the saving of American lives achieved by the sudden use of atomic bombs against Japan may be outweighed by the ensuing loss of confidence and by a wave of horror and revulsion sweeping over the rest of the world."

Taking all this into account, the report recommended that the new weapon be demonstrated before the world, to be witnessed by representatives of the United Nations. The test bombing would be held on a barren island with appropriate safeguards.

What was happening was that the scientists were looking ahead, bearing in mind that the war with Germany was over and that we were already closing in for the kill in Japan; looking ahead and trying to anticipate the nature of the problem of world control of atomic energy after the war was over; looking ahead and trying to establish a sound basis for international agreement creating reliable safeguards.

"The best possible atmosphere for the achievement of an international agreement could be achieved if America could say to the world: 'You see what sort of weapon we had but did not use. We are ready to renounce its use in the future if other nations join us in this renunciation and agree to the establishment of an efficient international control.'

"After such a demonstration, the weapon might perhaps be used against Japan if the sanction of the United Nations (and of public opinion at home) were obtained, perhaps after a preliminary ultimatum to Japan to surrender or at least to evacuate certain regions as an alternative to their total destruction.

"This may sound fantastic, but in nuclear weapons we have something entirely new in order of magnitude of destructive power, and if we want to capitalize fully on the advantage their possession gives us, we must use new and imaginative methods."

Summing up, the scientists expressed their conviction that a unilateral approach to the dropping of the bomb, even apart from moral considerations, however overwhelming, would almost inevitably result in unilateral action by other nations. And unilateralism in an atomic age was not merely a problem but a fatal disease. We would be undermining a possible common ground upon which common controls might later be built. As a corollary, we would be destroying whatever stand we might later decide to take on outlawing the use of atomic weapons in warfare. It would be naïve to expect other nations to take such a plea seriously in view of our own lack of reticence in dropping the bomb when the war was on the very verge of being won without it.

Why, then, did we drop it? Or, assuming that the use of the bomb was justified, why did we not at least demonstrate its power in a test under the auspices of the U.N., on the basis of which an ultimatum would be issued to Japan—transferring the burden of responsibility to the Japanese themselves?

In speculating upon possible answers to these questions, some facts available since the bombing may be helpful. We now know, for example, that Russia was scheduled to come into the war against Japan by August 8, 1945. Russia had agreed at Yalta to join the fight against Japan ninety days after V-E Day. Going after the knockout punch, we bombed Hiroshima on August 6, Nagasaki on August 9. Russia came into the war on August 8, as specified.

Can it be that we were more anxious to prevent Russia from establishing a claim for full participation in the occupation against Japan than we were to think through the implications of unleashing atomic warfare? Whatever the answer, one thing seems likely: There was not enough time between July 16, when we knew at New Mexico that the bomb would work, and August 8, the Russian deadline date, for us to have set up the very complicated machinery of a test atomic bombing involving time-consuming problems of area preparations; invitations and arrangements for observers (the probability being that the transportation to the South Pacific would in itself exceed the time limit); issuance of an ultimatum and the conditions of fulfillment, even if a reply limit was set at only forty-eight hours or less—just to mention a few.

No; any test would have been impossible if the purpose was to knock Japan out before Russia came in—or at least before Russia could make anything other than a token of participation prior to a Japanese collapse.

Meanwhile, the evidence indicates that the Soviet Union was doing everything possible to prolong the war in the East, until such time as she could establish a claim on the occupation of Japan. Japan had transmitted a request to the Soviet Union in June, 1945, asking that Moscow lend its offices as intermediary to ascertain what peace terms the United States would be willing to offer. This request was not relayed to the United States.

Even before the shooting war had ended, the Cold War had begun.

It may be argued that the strategical maneuverings of the United States and the Soviet Union were justified, that what they did was a legitimate exercise of power politics in a rough-and-tumble world. So far as the U.S. itself was concerned, it may be said that it avoided a struggle for authority in Japan similar to what it has since experienced in Germany, and that, unless the U.S. came out of the war with a decisive balance of power over the Soviet Union, it would be in no position to checkmate Russian expansion.

There is a dangerous plausibility here—a plausibility as inseparable from the war system of sovereign nations as armaments are from armaments races. It is the plausibility of power politics, of action leading to reaction, reaction leading to counterreaction, and counterreaction leading to war; of competitive systems of security rather than of workable world organization. It is a plausibility that rests on the flat assumption that war is inevitable, and that the U.S. should fight it at a time and under terms advantageous to itself.

At the end of World War II, such "plausibilities" were rejected by those who felt that the big job was to avert the next war, rather than to win it. And they saw no way to avert the next war other than through a world organization having the power to back up its decisions by law and relying upon preponderant force as needed. Such an organization would attempt to dispose of the fear-begetting-fear, provocation-begetting-provocation cycle; and to substitute in its place a central authority from which no member could withdraw or secede under any circumstances. It would automatically deprive potential aggressors of their traditional excuse for aggression—namely, their own encirclement and insecurity—and be strong enough to deal with them should a real threat arise.

It is possible, perhaps probable, that at the start not all nations would have been willing to join such an authority, but so long as the overwhelming majority was willing to establish it, it might have been only a matter of time before the others would have found it impossible to remain apart. Even if we assume that a nation continued to stand aloof, the question for the rest of the world was whether that nation represented more of a threat outside a system of world law than under world lawlessness.

Meanwhile, no such world law existed, and the United States, which was in the best position to make the initial proposals looking toward the development of the United Nations into an authority with responsible and adequate power, was taking no such initiative. It seemed content to see the U.N.—born so auspiciously and with such high hope—grow weaker day by day for want of nourishing authority to deal with the very question that gave it its main reason for being. True, David had only a slingshot, but the U.N. lacked even that in a world of push-button atomic warfare. There were no world police, no world agency with authority over the international instruments of death, no world law.

It is a harsh but necessary truth that the U.N., as constituted at San Francisco, was incapable of resolving major disputes among the major nations. Not that the U.N. has not since been given big jobs to do. No organization so weak has ever had thrust upon it problems so vast. But while the nations were generous in turning over their problems, they were niggardly in turning over the necessary authority. Time by itself would not cause the U.N. to grow and become strong. Only the nations could give it that growth. For the desperate necessity was to provide the U.N. with authority adequate to the problems of atomic energy or any other world problems too big for any single state to handle.

There was nothing abnormal in the crisis confronting the world at the end of World War II, any more than there would have been anything abnormal about a crime wave if all courts and police forces were abolished. And it would have been foolish to expect the crisis to solve itself and the threat of war to dry up and blow away so long as peoples failed to create law or even move toward world law.

There was the implied notion that the peace of the world could be assured if only a way could be found of handling or disposing of the Russian problem. The definite impression was given that one nation and one nation alone held the key to enduring peace. Without belittling the size of the crisis between the Soviet and the Anglo-American peoples, and without condoning aggression, threats, or iron curtains, it was hard to believe that any one nation, by behaving properly, could create a lasting peace.

Let us assume, for purposes of argument, that the earth opened up and swallowed the entire Soviet Union, and that world communism as a threat was swallowed up at the same time. Would the threat of war or the causes of war have disappeared as well? If so, how are we to explain the fact that Europe has been chewed up by war almost continually since there was a Europe to fight over—for centuries before anyone ever heard of Lenin or Stalin? How are we to account for the innumerable wars between England and France at such cost to both? How are we to account for World War I—or even World War II for that matter? And how can we be certain that the same causes might not result in a Russia-less World War III?

No; Russian unilateralism was not *the* disease; it was the *product* of the disease. Not *the* problem, but *part* of the problem. That problem was the centuries-old problem of competitive national sovereignties, as Mr. Emery Reves demonstrated so cogently in *The Anatomy of Peace*. That problem involved the race for security, each nation deciding for itself what was necessary for its own security, with the result that two or more nations would mark out the same areas as its exclusive security zones. That problem involved the setting up of military bases and the conversion of small nations into buffer states, with spheres of influence extending everywhere. That problem involved jockeying for position and power, with military alliances and blocs of states arrayed against each other. That problem involved reliance upon national military establishments, leading inevitably to an armaments race and, equally inevitably, to the use of those armaments.

Perhaps this is oversimplifying the problem and giving it too much of a pat approach. But if the big job before us at the end of World War II was the building of a peace that would free the world of war for the first time, since nothing less would be able to keep the human race alive, then it is necessary to define the problem for what it is.

Either world problems will be settled through *real* world organization, meaning world law, or they will be settled by world war. World law is not the end but the means. It is no distant goal but a present indispensable. It is not a hope but the *only* hope, the only chance. To whatever extent we delay, to whatever extent we move in other directions, by that much do we acquiesce with chaos.

VII. *The Fallacy of the Deterrent*

WE will not find the answer to nuclear war solely by contemplating its obscenity or horror or cost. Most people no longer have to be persuaded about the grim totality of nuclear war; they want to know how to avert it. And they want to be certain that they don't have to give up their liberties or their ideas in exchange.

This, then, is the real difficulty, rather than any inability necessarily to comprehend the nuclear reality. People properly feel that bemoaning a nuclear war is not a policy in itself; and they don't want to lose other things worth holding while embracing the cause of peace.

It is not enough, therefore, to shudder over pictures of bloated bodies floating up on a beach, or of maggoted corpses piled up like cordwood. All the poetic fervor in the world against war will not abolish war if men do not understand how wars begin and how peace must be made. Indeed, it has happened that a sense of horror alone may actually be a part of a drift toward war. Never before in history was there such a grandiose campaign to make people literate about the horrors of war as existed in this country during the period from 1919 to 1939. Hemingway, Dos Passos, and Remarque were only a few of the novelists who contributed to what amounted to a national conviction that if only we could squirm enough, we would never again have to fight.

The mood in the twenties and thirties was shaped in large part by disillusion. The dominant feeling, especially among young people, was that war was a matter of convenience and profit for the merchants of death. Books told of the machinations and manipulations of the munitions makers. Large advertisements dramatized the futility of war and the high cost of war. People really didn't die for their ideals in war; they merely sacrificed the ideals on the altar of power and profit.

While all this was going on, the nation that lost World War I was listening to different speeches and reading different books. The German people, or at least a substantial portion of them, were listening to Adolf Hitler. They listened to talk of manifest destiny, of opportunity to wipe out past defeats, of enemies within and without who had to be punished and expunged, of the need for force and the glory of force.

In the United States, people were reading powerful advertisements against war put out by World Peaceways; in Germany, people were at work in the armaments factories. As the military power of Nazi Germany rose, so did the provocations and the tensions. The fact that many people in America and Europe believed in the importance of peace and in the horror of war did not induce Germany to keep the peace. Indeed, the inability of other nations to defend themselves cost them their independence and the freedom of their peoples.

It was inevitable that this experience should have registered deeply with the peoples of Europe and the United States. The conditioned reflexes produced by that period were to create the mood and policies for the period following the end of World War II. In the United States especially, the response to any uncertainty or potential danger was to do the things that the nation had failed to do in response to the danger of the thirties.

It is natural, therefore, that many people should react to the threat of nuclear warfare by asking whether anything other than military preparedness can give them security.

Here we come to the basic difference between the situation before World War II and the situation today. Military power is *no longer* an adequate shield for the protection of national independence and individual freedoms.

A nation no longer "defends" itself by hurling back the aggressor. There is no known method by which one nation can physically restrain another nation from exploding its cities and expunging the lives of large numbers of its citizens. The best a nation can do is to threaten a devastating counterattack.

In today's world, the only possible function of military preparedness is to prevent war—without losing those things for which a nation would have fought in the past. For the moment war breaks out, no matter how complete the military preparedness may have been, the military policy has failed. Its principal function will have been shattered— along with everything else.

Conventional ideas of defending the homeland and preserving its values are meaningless. Of all the implications of atomic energy, none is more basic than this. And that is why the theory of the deterrent offers no reasonable hope of protecting a nation, its people, its freedoms.

At the heart of the deterrent theory, of course, is the belief that a potential enemy will be disinclined to attack if he knows the counterattack will be immediate and devastating. Advocates of the deterrent idea also contend that the nation's military potential must in no way be modified or hindered by agreements on arms control or disarmament. Similarly, they regard any security activities of a world organization that impinge upon a nation's freedom of action in the field of arms and power as undesirable. Thus, restrictions on nuclear testing or the development of missiles are generally considered inconsistent with the requirements of a nation's security.

The main flaw in the deterrent theory, however, is that it does not deter. The possession by the Soviet Union of advanced nuclear weapons has not served as a deterrent to the United States in matters involving national interests. The United States has not allowed fear of nuclear weapons to deter it from making clear that it was prepared to fight with everything it had to keep from being pushed out of Berlin. Each has attempted to convince the other that it is prepared to let fly with everything it owns rather than back down.

It is natural for a nation to display not restraint but willingness to march to the brink when its national interests are threatened. Even when the threat is not a major one, there is a natural concern lest an unchallenged small threat lead to a larger one. In a world of anarchy, not deterrents but the compulsions of national sovereignty are the prime movers.

The announcement by one nation that it has achieved a military breakthrough in one field creates in the other nation not a mood of defeat but a blistering determination to match that particular weapon and surpass it. The United States possessed an atomic monopoly from 1945 to 1948. This period of monopoly coincided with the period of maximum Soviet aggressiveness and intransigence. Similarly, the advent of the Soviet sputnik, with its portents of long-range rockets carrying nuclear bombs, did not cause the United States to ask for surrender terms. What it did was to light fires of determination in the United States to close the gap.

One nation's deterrent becomes the other nation's incentive. The fact of Soviet rocket supremacy led to various extreme counterproposals from the American military, by way of bolstering the deterrent against surprise attack. One such proposal called for hundreds of American jet planes, fully loaded with nuclear explosives, to be in the air at all times and within ready striking distance of the Soviet Union. The object would be to avoid the destruction of U.S. retaliatory capacity through a sudden attack and to ensure the mobility of its striking force.

The practical effect of such a move, however, could be exactly the opposite from the one intended. First, the fact of hundreds of jet planes in the air could lead to even more extreme counter-measures. One could be in the form of dozens of earth-circling satellites, each loaded with hydrogen bombs. Another could take the form of high-speed submarines only a few hundred miles off the East and West coasts of the United States, each of them equipped with launching platforms for missiles carrying nuclear explosives.

Each side, as noted earlier, would have to reckon with the risk that a pilot or submarine commander might go berserk and make the decision that would start the full chain reaction. The possibility of an accident or a miscalculation would grow in direct proportion to the distribution of the power and the means of instant use.

The spiraling competition for military advantage carries with it ascending and accelerating tensions. Fear of surprise attack is the greatest single factor in the thinking and planning of the opposing military strategists. The pressure is building up in each country to hit first rather than wait to be hit. The same logic that gave birth to the around-the-clock jet bomber and the nuclear-cocked satellite will argue that there is no choice except to take the final initiative. Thus, the deterrent leads to preventive or pre-emptive war. Since the opposing countries have to contend with the same factors in surprise nuclear attack, each knows the other is considering the same antidotes; the very fact that each is even considering preventive war causes the other to move in that direction itself.

The incredible paradox is that both potential foes today seek security in the same terms. Each calls upon the other to be deterred by its striking power, yet both are becoming more insecure in direct proportion to the increase in their own power.

The theory of the deterrent marks the ultimate failure of unfettered national determination in an internationally anarchic world. Never in history has the sovereign state been more powerful or less secure. Its capacity for waging war has never been so great, nor its ability to protect itself so puny. In turning to the theory of the deterrent for protection, it invokes irrational force as the principal means of creating rational restraint. Far from inspiring great restraints, the deterrent produces jitters and hair triggers.

What is most significant about the policy of the military deterrent is that it is the lineal descendant of a long series of failures.

The first policy failure grew out of the assumption that the United States enjoyed an atomic monopoly that would last far longer than it actually did. The military head of the atomic energy project testified before a Congressional committee that the Soviet Union would be unable to make an atomic bomb of its own for perhaps twenty years, if indeed then. Substantially disregarded were the stern warnings of nuclear scientists that there were no "secrets." There were mammoth difficulties that only a highly industrialized society with an advanced technology could meet. But these difficulties were not insuperable for a major nation.

When the predictions of the scientists turned out to be correct in this respect, the policy of "secrecy" and "monopoly" was succeeded by a policy of supremacy. It was felt that the United States could stay far ahead in the nuclear race. But the Soviet Union very early developed a high-megaton thermonuclear weapon and sprang into a substantial lead with long-range missiles.

The response to this by the United States was "massive retaliation" to dissuade any aggressor. But this was like threatening mutual suicide. Moreover, it was never too clear whether the retaliation would be invoked if the United States were directly attacked or if trouble flared up anywhere in the world. If the latter, there might be some doubt about its precise origins.

In any event, other nations expressed profound concern about the implications of this policy and it seemed to recede, at least so far as the term "massive retaliation" was concerned. In its place came the new term "military deterrent." But all the elements of inadequacy that characterized the progenitors were present in the offspring.

There is yet another fallacy to the deterrent theory. It assumes a static world. It assumes that everything will be kept under tight control, that upheavals in the making for more than a century will somehow remain quiescent. It does not take into account that the nuclear deterrent will not prevent social and political unrest and the consequent disturbance of the peace. People who have great grievances will be in the market for revolution until the grievances are met. The quest for independence and yearnings of the majority of the world's peoples will not take an indefinite holiday. Basic forces such as these will become violent if the means for effective peaceful change are lacking. The U.S. will not keep Communist or other ideologies from exploiting those forces just by calling attention to its nuclear deterrent. If it wants to be effective in these situations, it shall have to come up with some relevant ideas.

The basic problem is with the concept "national security." The term has a built-in contradiction. In the atomic age, no national security is possible. Either there is a workable world security system or there is nothing. Indeed, the efforts of the individual nations to achieve military supremacy or even adequacy are actually competitive and provocative in their effects.

Such being the case, how does a nation protect itself against aggression? How does it safeguard its freedom and its values?

The best chance—perhaps its only chance—for meeting these needs is through the development of a common security. The people who settled frontier territory found that the only workable answer to lawlessness was the adequate machinery of law. A single individual, no matter how well armed, was unable to defend himself and his family. Only as enough individuals, acting together to create a consensus, also created specific machinery to deal with the anarchy, did the anarchy subside. It is substantially the same in the world today. Only as the world's peoples see beyond the limitations of absolute sovereignty will they be able to deal with the volatile actions of the nations in the world arena.

A common security requires machinery. It requires new rules of the game. It requires new conditionings, new habits, new outlooks, new prospects, new allegiances. The new allegiances need not eliminate the old. They need only take into account the oldest fact in the world; namely, that man has the obligation to create a sane society for himself and to safeguard the essential conditions of his well-being.

Control over weapons of mass destruction will not by itself create or maintain peace. But it may well be the best place to take hold in any attempt to build a durable peace. And it can eliminate at least that aspect of the danger that stems from nuclear jitters over fear of surprise attack. It serves as a sort of ground-clearing operation for the numberless things that must follow if the peace is to be real. Without it, the cause of peace is almost certainly lost.

Yet if nothing happens beyond disarmament, then it may be only a matter of time before the same uncertainties and apprehensions that caused the nations to arm in the first place would reassert themselves. Indeed, there is no point in disarming unless something is done to eliminate the original tensions or areas of insecurity.

Therefore, the key question about disarmament has to do with ultimate purpose. What kind of peace are we trying to create? What kind of security system will take the place of arms? Under what circumstances can people feel reasonably secure against aggression and surprise attack? In short, what is the long-range, broad-gauge program of which disarmament is an initial part?

The answer must lie in the establishment of an authority which takes away from nations, summarily and completely, not only the machinery of battle that can wage war, but the machinery of decision that can start a war. The United Nations is not yet that kind of authority. The main job before the world is to make it one.

VIII. *Two Kinds of Sovereignty*

THE business of coping with bullies comes close to being the oldest business in the world. Most men have neither the desire nor stomach for altercation or domination. Those who do have frequently been able to prey on the others. Sometimes, as in the days of the American West, the bullies would put themselves above the law, using guns as the source of both authority and immunity.

The individual may have been no match for the bully; but several hundred men could come together and make the decisions that would provide for the common safety. They could draw up the rules of the game, designate those who would have the authority to carry arms, and establish qualified men to guard against the abuse of power. In this way, through law, the weak became strong and the reign of bullies was ended.

In a curious sense, the advent of total power has pushed the entire human race back to the time when men were at the mercy of bullies; that is, a time when government either did not exist or was incapable of dealing with lawlessness. The dominant condition of mankind is anarchy. Whatever the present forms of law and order in the world may be, they have only limited validity. For these forms exist only inside the nation. But the overriding danger to life comes from the absence of authority over the nation itself. In the absence of a higher tribunal, a nation interprets for itself the requirements of justice. It inevitably pursues its own self-interest in contact with other nations. And a nation knows no law except self-determination. But the self-determination of one nation is the anarchy of all. And the ultimate consequences of world anarchy for the individual are even more menacing than they would be inside the nation itself. For the end product of world anarchy could mean the end of the age of man, whereas anarchy inside the nation might inflict its harm only on a limited number.

The individual in today's world, therefore, can no longer look to the nation as the main source of his security. It is able no longer to protect him against invasion or assault from other nations. It is able no longer to furnish the main conditions of his growth or to safeguard his values or institutions or culture or property. No matter how wide the oceans that surround the nation, no matter how bristling its defenses, its people are totally vulnerable to shattering attack. The nation possesses retaliatory power, true, but even in the exercise of that power it engages in a form of self-assault, for power is directed against the delicate and precarious conditions that make existence possible, and, indeed, against the mainstream of life itself.

This is the central, overwhelming fact about the twentieth century. The fully sovereign nation has become separated from its historic reason for being. It is not only incapable of protecting the lives, values, and property of its citizens; it has actually become inimical to life and creative freedom.

It is inimical because it is violating the natural rights of man. These natural rights are above the rights of the state and should be beyond the reach and the authority of the state. The good society exists to serve and protect these rights. Man has a right to keep himself from being cheapened, debased, or deformed. He has a right to creative growth. He has a right to individual sanctity and sovereignty. He has a right to make life purposeful. If these natural rights should die, though human flesh in some form remain, then the survivors will not be the lucky ones.

The rights of the state are many. They include the right to sacrifice human life or to take human life in the defense of the nation. But there is nothing in the political rights of the state or its rulers that includes the right to strike at the nature of man or to disfigure the face of man or to toy with the vital balances that make life possible.

The state is so busy fending for itself in the great open arena where nations come into contact with each other, jostling or preening or jockeying for position, that all other functions become secondary. And the insecure state tends to bolster its position by doing the things that add to the insecurity of the individual. It does this through standing armies or increased taxes or a prodded economy or internal security measures that reflect and increase the many tensions they try to eliminate.

If the states live in anarchy the individual citizen pays the price of anarchy. Law and order within the state are no protection against the larger violence and injustice outside the state. Whatever the intermediate forms of protection afforded to man in his daily life, the major threats to his well-being and future find him open and exposed.

All this the state does in the name of security. If this is what total sovereignty has come to mean, then it is a monstrous thing and man has the duty to replace it with the higher and saner forms that conflict neither with nature itself nor his own natural rights.

Not only is there no conflict between peace and freedom; the same measures required to establish a just and proper peace make possible the existence of a creative freedom. Just as absolute sovereignty today is incapable of producing peace, so it is incapable of ensuring freedom. To the extent that a nation looks to its own absolute sovereignty to achieve security and maintain freedom, it weakens both. In short, the absolute sovereign state is a flimsy shelter for a free society.

No matter how hard today's sovereign state tries to pursue security through power, the power is never quite enough. For other states are increasing their power too. The state and its people are thus trapped in their own sovereign coils. To have no power when other nations are becoming powerful could be an invitation to attack and disaster. But the pursuit of power means the pursuit of superior power, hard to define and even harder to create.

The dilemma is especially acute for free peoples. They have been vulnerable to aggressors in the past precisely because their freeness makes for openness. And, even as they now accept the need to become brawny in the cause of self-preservation, they become involved in something beyond their control—a massive competition in potential terror the very nature of which pulls them inexorably toward a showdown.

For the dictator state the world condition of tension and uncertainty offers a natural habitat. The presence or prospect of an outer threat lends weight to the internal controls. But even if the dictatorship faces the stark need for changes inside itself; even if it is willing to denounce or renounce its own tyrants and the products of the tyranny; even if it is willing to modify its ideological ambitions for large dominion—even if it does all these things the mountain of its sovereign statehood still stands. The sovereignty precedes the ideology and indeed survives it. And in its sovereign role the dictator state sticks to its last. It may make concessions, it may permit deviations, but it will not surrender its position above the law. As it concerns the ultimate question of national sovereignty, it insists on the unlimited and unfettered development and mobilization of its own power.

How, then, is the wall of unfettered sovereignty to be

broken? If the free state is reluctant to accept higher controls, and the unfree state is adamant against those controls, where do we look for safety and sanity?

It becomes necessary, then, for the nation to develop new means of performing its historic role. If the existence of force can no longer serve as the main source of a nation's security, something else will have to take its place if human society is to be able to endure and function.

As with an individual or group confronted by the bully, the need is for enough people to come together to determine how to protect themselves in the light of existing conditions, and how to establish whatever new approaches or agencies may be required for the common safety. The new power that must be brought into being is power in its most natural form. It is the power represented by human will— the power of consensus. Out of it can come the energy and momentum for building a new flooring for human society. Out of it, too, can come workable checks on heretofore uncontrolled force—all as part of a system of justice in the intercourse of nations.

This leads to a paradox. The individual wants to create something beyond the nation that can give him the protections once afforded by the nation, yet the nation itself is his only instrumentality for achieving it. The only place an individual can find firm footing for a stand is inside a nation; how, therefore, can he be effective outside the nation?

Just as there is a concept of natural law that transcends the state, so there is a concept of natural will that can transcend the nation. A new force that is emerging in the world is the force of world public opinion. It is as yet without formal channels or organs of expression. No matter; it is a developing new power and it is becoming increasingly audible. Public opinion inside the nation is at its most powerful when it is concerned with questions of justice or overriding moral issues. Similarly, world public opinion can make its power felt on the big questions that have moral content or that are concerned with the rational means of safeguarding human life.

No freedom is more meaningful for the individual of a free society than to use that freedom in a cause that is not confined to the nation. He can use his footing inside the nation to work for a consensus inside the nation, one that can lead to effective commitments by the nation to an ordered society.

Do these commitments mean the end of national sovereignty?

Not necessarily; they need mean only the end of *absolute* national sovereignty.

For there are two kinds of sovereignty. One is absolute. The other is relative.

Absolute sovereignty means that a nation will not submit itself to the *compulsory* jurisdiction of a world body in matters concerned with world disputes or problems; will not subordinate its military policy to a world body; will not agree in advance to a set of rules for world law under which its only recourse is a world court. In short, absolute sovereignty means that a state may be willing to negotiate on a treaty basis, but insists on the right of revocation as circumstances may warrant.

Relative sovereignty means that a state can retain jurisdiction over its way of life. The force available to it is ample for purposes of internal security and development, but not for external aggression or conquest. The nature of nuclear weapons makes it possible to draw a line between the two. A nation does not need nuclear weapons to maintain law and order among its citizens, or even to deal with the threat of armed insurrection. Weapons adapted to mass destruction can therefore be removed from the jurisdiction of the nation and placed under the control of the world organization.

In a world without absolute national sovereignty, the world organization can underwrite national independence and relative sovereignty. It is not necessary for the nation to be dissolved in order to create a situation of safety on earth. It is necessary only for national sovereignty to be made meaningful, to eliminate those attributes of it that add up to world anarchy, and to assure and underwrite those attributes that add up to national responsibility.

It is possible, indeed, that only by eliminating absolute sovereignty can meaningful sovereignty or independence be maintained. For security depends on a world organization with adequate power to exercise workable control of the destructive weapons, cope with tensions that could lead to conflict, provide a basis for justice in the increasingly complex dealings of nations, attack the basic causes of war, and set up an instrumentality for justice.

We are living, all of us—whether Americans, Russians, English, French, Chinese, Lebanese, Egyptians, or Siamese —in two totally different worlds.

The first of these worlds is old, familiar, visible, combustible, and unworkable. It is the world in which nations act as nations have always acted. Experience has taught them that they live a hazardous and unpredictable existence; that life is full of sneak attacks and that anything they own may suddenly be taken from them. And so, they insist on the means of producing and inflicting mass death. They attempt to maintain security through strength. If that strength is insufficient, they try to combine it with the strength of other nations when there is an identity of interests. Since they operate in a world without law, security is a matter of individual definition.

There are principles of action and strategy in this world, but they are not always consistent with abstract moral principles or what it is that serves the ends and needs of a human individual and enables him to grow and to be truly free.

The question of morality in such a world is irrelevant because morality cannot exist where a perpetual clash of interests is assumed and where brute force determines the ultimate shape of history.

It is quite logical that a nation should act to protect its self-interests in a world of conflicting national interests—a world in which the struggle for power is real and in which force has been used repeatedly to assert the national will.

Now we come to the second world. It is new, complex, exacting, difficult; it is also at once dangerous and promising. The second world is one of almost total change. It has changed the physical earth in its relationship to man. Vast distances have ceased to exist. The new reach and power of human beings know almost no tangible limits. Most important of all is that nuclear switches can now be pulled and whole nations and their peoples expunged from the face of the earth. There is also the prospect of an ultimate switch, soon to be created if it does not already exist, that can burn all life off the planet.

Such a new world imposes stern conditions. It requires a high order of intelligence. It cannot be subjected to unlimited strains or tensions. It will not operate itself. It must be operated; but the people who operate it must know what they are doing. In this sense it is as exacting and demanding and difficult as the highest science.

The principal stress point in such a world is absolute national sovereignty. And it is at this point that the two worlds, old and new, come into conflict. However logical and natural it may seem to a nation to assert its sovereignty through force or a show of force inside the old world of plot-and-counter-plot, self-interest, and balance of power, the changed conditions of the new world make absolute national sovereignty unworkable. Military victory, the supreme achievement of sovereignty, is no longer possible. Nations no longer declare war or wage war; they declare or wage mutual suicide.

The kind of action, therefore, that only a few years ago would have seemed proper and inevitable for a nation to take in pursuit of its self-interest no longer makes sense. Indeed, it can be the quickest way of putting a nuclear match to the planet.

We exist in two different worlds but we pay a price for it. Decisions may be made on the level of old-world thinking but the consequences take place in the new. A nation that is guided primarily by traditional ideas of self-interest may quickly discover it will lose its principal power. For real power in the new world is measured by the leadership a nation is able to exert among the large majority of the peoples on earth, by its moral standing, by its ability to recognize new realities, by its desire not to use force but to control it, by its willingness to work for a true rule of law in the world and the means to enforce it.

Living in this new world does not mean we ignore the existence of threatening ideologies. It simply means we have to fashion new ways of competing with those ideologies. For Americans or Russians, it means they can challenge each other to the most important competition of all —a competition in service to the human community. It is possible that victory is to be found on this level and on none other. Since raw force defeats its own purpose, it becomes necessary to develop the new approaches and ideas that happen to fit the new age. If Americans are seriously concerned about the threat of communism in the world, they will invest themselves and their resources in a total commitment to the cause of a better and safer world. They won't store or destroy their surplus wheat but use it in the war against hunger. They won't grumble about the veto in the U.N., which they themselves sponsored, but will proclaim their readiness to be part of a U.N. without a veto and with the authority to enforce world law. They won't attempt to improvise a police force for the U.N. on an emergency basis on matters affecting their national interests, but will advocate the need for a permanent U.N. force—adequate to deter aggression, adequate to carry out inspection as part of workable control over nuclear arms, adequate to keep the peace itself.

These are some of the basic requirements imposed by the new world. An individual citizen of a nation does not serve the cause of his country just by cheering for his side every time it sends men with guns into other countries in an effort to protect its self-interest. For ultimate security depends not so much on the give-and-take of conflicting national self-interests as it does on the response of peoples to the challenge of the new world. Now is the time for all men to come to the aid of the human party, and to create a situation of sanity and safety in the world. This may enable the individual to be secure in the only way it is possible for him to be secure.

IX. *En Route to a True Civilization*

WHEN men turn to history, they become self-congratulatory. They identify themselves with the great names in human experience; they give themselves credit for having produced a Galileo or a Harvey or a Lavoisier or a Jefferson.

But such self-esteem is a form of self-delusion. Galileo's researches and conclusions did not bring about a race of men uniformly capable of peering into the nature of the universe as he had done. The overwhelming majority of men continued as they were. Harvey's discoveries about human blood did not transform all doctors into his intellectual counterparts; they may have learned about the bloodstream and improved their ability to diagnose and treat; but there were vast remaining areas in which their own natural limitations gave continued shelter to dangerous nonsense about the treatment of human disease. Lavoisier changed man's notions about chemistry and helped to make it into a science, but this did not mean that everyone in chemistry, much less in the human family, was suddenly brought up to his level of intelligence.

It is a colossal conceit to suppose that the sharing of knowledge or techniques automatically produces a sharing of greatness. To be the beneficiary of an idea is not quite the same as originating it. Also, to have reached a peak in some fields today does not necessarily mean that civilization is now at a pinnacle from which man can look back upon and down upon long ages of mass delusion. We live a life of compartmentalization; some sections are marked with glittering splendor; others are as dimly lighted as they were thousands of years ago. We are still bound to dangerously primitive ideas.

Indeed, the most primitive idea ever entertained by the mind of man persists in our own age. It is not the notion that people are pursued by evil spirits and that these have to be cast out, whether through the sacrifice of things or of human life.

Nor is it the belief, held in many parts of the Western world at various times during the fourteenth through six-teenth centuries, that the Devil had his agents on earth, and that this evil has to be extirpated through human hanging or burning.

Nor the belief in the philosopher's stone or in miracle mediums that do everything—from transmuting objects into pure gold to endowing human beings with eternal youth.

Nor even the belief that man has divine sanction to spread his religion at the point of a sword, resulting in the spilled blood of millions of resisters and of almost equal numbers of converters.

The most primitive and dangerous idea ever held by the mind of man is the notion that it is somehow possible to preserve human civilization on this earth in the present condition of world anarchy. It is the notion that no extraor-dinary measures are required to deal with the extraordi-nary situation of a world that has suddenly been compressed into a tight unit. At a time when weapons of absolute de-struction are poised for instant use, the bizarre belief exists that the human group can work its way out of crisis through measures that have never succeeded in the past.

Bemused or puzzled as modern man has been by popular delusions or irrational mass behavior of past ages, he himself is now contributing vast material for the bewilderment of future generations. For nothing in history can begin to compare with the present spectacle of a world drifting toward a possible war of hydrogen bombs with little general realization of the need for people to transcend their petty problems and dedicate themselves to the building of a structure of world law in time to prevent world war.

Meanwhile, many of the statesmen, philosophers, and theologians who should be taking the initiative in a titanic movement for sanity are exempting themselves from the moral responsibility of leadership. Privately they may be expressing their belief in the necessity for world law; publicly they are holding back because of the fear that the idea may be considered too visionary or even unrespectable. Or if they allow their private thoughts to spill over into public statements they do so tentatively and obscurely, hoping somehow to avoid any public intimation that they are actually saying what they are actually thinking. In this they have had a remarkable success; their ideas have been cauterized against greatness and against the very quality of open inspiration that people hunger for today.

It now seems incredible that at one time men like Sir Thomas Browne should have associated themselves with the persecution of "witches," or that men of the reputation of Roger Bacon and Paracelsus should have failed to declare themselves against sorcery and black magic. Yet distant generations may find it even stranger that men of standing in theology and philosophy should have spent their time spinning elaborate theories about the uniqueness of Western Civilization instead of pursuing the necessary philosophy of the whole. From that distant perspective it may be seen that some of our scholars and churchmen were locked deep within their own categories when they should have been trying to plumb and define the universals of human values that were at stake in the crisis of the twentieth century. For what is most important about Western Civilization is its capacity for change and surprise; and what is most important about Eastern Civilization is its unchartable diversity. It may later be seen that whatever was good in both civilizations could have been saved only through common recognition of common goals.

In the past the world didn't merely slough off its primitive ideas or stumble out of them. The defeat of a delusion was generally the result of courageous response to courageous leadership. Not infrequently what would happen was that a few great men were unafraid to appeal directly to the good sense and quality of integrity that are deep within most men and that have only to be awakened in order to constitute the strongest force known in history. The great men who made these appeals were not concerned with the safety or respectability of their reputations—as reputations were measured in their own time. Nor were they seeking personal glory. They were seeking the end of delusion or of evil. They became great because they knew how to summon people to greatness.

If the pathetic fallacy of the twentieth century—the fallacy that law among nations is neither possible nor desirable—is to be destroyed, it may need some open thinking and speaking. The capacity of people to respond to that type of leadership may be greater than the nominal leaders think. A generation that is anticipating a rendezvous with destiny deserves and needs to be challenged.

Another primitive aspect of contemporary life is that the most important job in the world is not being done by anyone on a full-time basis.

Many weird things emerge from history, but it is doubtful whether any of them can compare with the absence of men in positions of *authority* to perform the most vital functions of all.

People devote full time to planting, building, sweeping, cleaning, carving, cooking, directing, or playing. They give full time to food, animals, papers, machines, human problems. And they are certainly giving full time to fashioning the enormously efficient weapons that will be used if the peace should fail.

Where is the man who is giving full time to the making of workable peace?

Is it argued that the Secretary General and his colleagues of the United Nations are hired for this express purpose?

The Secretary General has a vastly difficult and important job, which he handles well. But he is necessarily submerged in copious administrative work and detail. Even more basic is the fact that the nations he has to serve have defined his job in a way that keeps him from attacking the problem at its largest. The nations have insisted on retaining for themselves ultimate authority in matters of security. They want the right to possess greater physical force than they are willing to invest in the organization charged with the maintenance of world peace. They have provided no specific or adequate machinery to prevent aggression.

Is it argued that the President of the United States or the British Prime Minister or the Indian Prime Minister or other leading statesmen are devoting full time to the biggest job in the world? These men and others are making substantial contributions to the peace; but all one has to do is to consult the daily calendars of these men to see how their time is consumed. The papers that pass over their desks, the political problems involved in the running of a state, the endless procession of people whose importance must be acknowledged—all these get in the way.

Is it argued that the U.S. Secretary of State or the foreign ministers of the various nations are full-time employees whose job it is to safeguard human existence? The very nature of a foreign minister's job might almost be said to preclude the kind of service to the human community that is needed today. Basically, he is guardian of the national sovereignty. He engages in the diplomatic warfare. His official duties may lead him in the opposite direction from what is now required, which is to create an authority over the nation itself.

If the War Against Man should occur, it will come about not because it is inevitable but because not enough men have taken the trouble to avert it. It will be a grim reflection not on the inexorability of history but on the low value we place on the uniqueness of human life.

It might help, too, if somewhere there would emerge a man who felt as deeply about the entire human community as Gandhi felt about the people of India, a man of towering moral stature and imagination whose goodness and willingness to sacrifice himself in the cause of man would be universally recognized. The power of his compassion might be enough to shatter the sovereignty of violence on earth.

The central fact about leadership in the present world crisis is that it tends to respond rather than initiate. When the clamor is strong enough, there are important stirrings in high directions. But the powerful thrust toward the making of a safer and better world may have to come from outside officialdom. Few developments in recent history are more significant, in fact, than that the designated leadership has virtually exempted itself from any great design for human survival.

Consider, for example, the recurrent failures of high-level meetings of statesmen. In themselves, they are symptomatic of the larger failure; namely, the failure to think in terms of historical principle. Certainly, even heated discussions are preferable to nuclear confrontation. But summit conferences tend to be ends in themselves, rather than means to ends. The agenda is generally concerned with keeping immediate serious problems from reaching the blister stage. Yet what is needed is a new mechanism that can render last-minute summit conferences unnecessary. Talking is always better than shooting, but if the men who do the talking are unable to commit themselves to basic changes in the relationships of their nations to one another, then they may postpone a showdown but they may not necessarily avert it.

No single lesson in history was more urgent to the men who met in Philadelphia in 1787 than that peace is too important to be left to last-minute conferences. There was no place in their thinking for the notion that the most essential work in the world could be hastily improvised by political chieftains who had been riding hard all along in different directions. The genius of the Constitution-makers was that they read themselves out of the picture. They fitted themselves into something larger and more durable than an *ad hoc* approach to survival and freedom. That larger something was a Constitutional framework of law in which all men, including the heads of the states themselves, had specific obligations. And along with the obligations went firm limitations on the power of individuals.

The American federation-makers placed their reliance not on the variable moods of men but on the rules of the game and the machinery that could make it work. Not that human agencies could be dispensed with; even laws had to be interpreted and enforced by men. But laws at least defined the standard and supplied the yardsticks of justice. Without laws each man would be his own court and enforcement agency. This would incline him to conflict as naturally as he would start up at a strange sound in the dark. Law might not always work. It might be corrupted or distorted, but that only emphasized the need to restore it and bolster it, and not to dispense with it.

To repeat: summit meetings can reduce tensions. They can result in mutual pledges to abstain from further development or manufacture of the continental pulverizing explosives. These pledges might even be backed up by agreements to make each nation accessible to inspectors from other nations. All this is helpful, but it doesn't meet the problem where the problem exists. The real problem is not agreement or treaty but law. It is the kind of law that operates under a sovereignty of its own in the area of world peace. It requires a specific structure of world organization which is not subordinate to the individual nations in matters of arms control or world security. It inspects and enforces not because it is permitted to do so but because that is its clearly defined job. It can use all the good will it can get but it doesn't count on it, and it can exercise its authority without it if it has to.

The heads of states are not to be blamed if their crisis meetings skirt the real problem. For they are themselves prisoners of the very sovereignty they have come to protect and preserve. Thus meetings at the top level tend to be limited to a reshuffling of old factors rather than the creation of the necessary new ones.

It might be useful for men at the summit to consider why a summit meeting should be necessary in the first place. If the machinery of the United Nations had been able to do the job intended for it, there would be no need for top-level meetings. If the U.N. is to survive, what is necessary is not so much the willingness of the individual nations to refer matters to the U.N. but the built-in authority of the U.N. that can act whether the nations like it or not. At present, the U.N. acts when it has the consent of the parties involved. Thus, it becomes an arbitration agency instead of a law-making and law-enforcing agency. Any policeman who is required to obtain the consent of a law-breaker before he, the policeman, can do his job is not a policeman but a supplicant. The men who lead the nations have the obligation to agree to a revision conference of the U.N. for the purpose of converting it from an arena of unlimited options to an organization of binding obligations.

Such a revision conference might in fact and in truth justify the use of the term "summit meeting." Its job will be to tame the nations, to define the principles of justice in the world, to bring under rigid control the nuclear arsenals, and to create the basis for the responsible administration of the affairs of the human community.

Even when we do all this, there is no guarantee that it will work. But it at least puts the resources of human intelligence and energy to work where they are most needed.

In order that binding commitments instead of tentative agreements be reached it may be essential to look beyond the emergency meetings to a full-scale convention of the nations. The agenda for such a convention would be swept clean of the usual items involving national prestige and power, thrust and counterthrust, plot and counterplot. There would be one major item on the agenda: The creation of a common authority with sovereignty of its own, responsible to the world's peoples, with enforceable powers over disarmament. In short, the agenda is survival.

If such powers existed in the United Nations today it would be neither necessary nor possible to summon a conference outside of it for the purpose of dealing with immediate threats to the peace. In fact, nothing more sharply dramatizes the nature of the present world anarchy than the fact that the U.N. is hardly even mentioned in the efforts to deal with such crises as Suez or Berlin.

No objection to the argument for enforceable world law is weaker than the one which says: "Sure, but how?" Adequate action begins with a declaration of intent. It advances through advocacy. It comes to life through special effort with some measure of dedication behind it. When this is done we will be in a position to estimate either the difficulties or the possibilities or both, but not before.

In our time it is not enough to convene the peak personalities. It becomes necessary to convene the peak ideas. Peace today is not to be found just by making a trip to some magic mountain, but in putting tall thoughts and purposes to work. The credentials of the participants must be represented not by their titles or ribbons but by their ability to create a totally new way of life among the nations.

X. *Peace Through the U.N.*

IT would be foolish to expect any single plan for a restructured United Nations to produce a panacea for global problems. But at least a beginning can be made in eliminating such basic weaknesses of the United Nations as may now be complicating world tensions. Structurally, one of the dangers of weak international organization is that it cannot provide adequate security for the individual nation, large or small. There is no real deterrent to aggression. Dynamic nations are tempted to exploit military vacuums wherever they can find them. Peace-loving nations are forced into elaborate armaments defense preparedness. It is only a matter of time before there is a scramble for power and a saturation of tensions.

The United Nations Charter anticipates the need for change in its own structure. It provides for a general review conference for the purpose of considering basic new facts that may affect the future of the U.N.

How would a revision conference go about acting on new facts? What are the general problems that would probably come before a review conference of the United Nations?

Fundamentally, of course, the basic purpose of a review conference would be to explore the means by which the United Nations could enact, enforce, and interpret the rule of law. Moreover, such a conference could offer the world a chance to wipe the slate clean. The benefits of participation in such a strengthened body should be equally available to all. Membership should be universal. Any nation sincerely interested in security and the common welfare of the world's peoples should have no hesitation in joining with the rest.

There are benefits, but there are also obligations and responsibilities. The durable, meaningful peace to which humanity is entitled cannot be obtained without sacrifice.

The conditions for membership can be clearly stated: respect for the rules of the game, respect for the rights of the individual members, prompt fulfillment of obligations, recognition that the human community has precedence over the national community in those specific matters related to a common world security.

The United Nations is not a country club or a fraternal order. It should exist for the purpose of defining the obligations of nations and enforcing them. The more recalcitrant a nation, the more of a problem it represents to world order, the greater the need to have it within the jurisdiction of an ordered world. But universal membership in a U.N. also presupposes responsible authority on those matters affecting the peace.

The aim of a revised U.N., then, would be to have its own actual and potential forces, large enough to prevent aggression or to cope with it instantly if it should occur. As said earlier, it should be able to legislate effectively in the matter of national armaments; which is to say, the world's peoples must have confidence in the disarmament arrangements. It should enjoy the right of inspection to guard against secret manufacture of weapons adapted to mass destruction.

What sovereign rights ought the nations to retain? The individual nations have a right to insist on recapturing sovereignty over their own institutions and cultures. I use the word "recapturing" because sovereignty in domestic matters has been seriously weakened under world anarchy, with war or the fear of war determining the careers and destinies of millions of citizens, the size of their taxes, or the pressures upon free institutions.

Because of the sheer weight and complexity of all these questions, there is a real danger that a review conference could fall apart almost at the start. That is why it is so important, before any specific matters of substance are discussed, that the conference recognize frankly its own inability to come up with definitive answers at a *single* session. There should be an orderly and progressive consideration of the problems without any time limit as to expiration date of the meetings. For the conference must be more than another international meeting; it should be a congress of history and hope, studying man's efforts to govern himself in units of increasing size and complexity. It requires the most painstaking scrutiny of the historical record; it must combine wisdom with knowledge, insight with information, vision with comprehension. Three or four years or more is not too long a time for such a service to the world community. The Philadelphia Convention of the American states took the better part of two years, and the public debate continued for years more.

In particular, in organizing its work over the long range, the conference could divide itself into various parts. The initial full session of the conference could be concerned with a general discussion of problems and objectives. After the preliminary meetings, the group could be narrowed down to a working committee, with every nation having at least a single representative. The group would meet regularly, with no fixed date for concluding its labors. At least twice a year, the full review conference could be reconvened for the purpose of receiving an interim report of the working committee and for advising the committee on the general pattern of its work.

The most difficult, yet most important, achievement of a working committee would no doubt be to suggest how the United Nations can have interim police powers until such time as the United Nations is invested with the general powers of world law. This may require a timetable for the execution of a four-phase plan for interim world security.

In the first phase of this timetable, the United Nations could be given command of military forces of at least three times the size of the forces it maintained at Korea. This might amount to approximately one million men under arms—a small figure as modern armies go but enough to serve symbolic purposes as well as to act as a deterrent for the type of aggression that, as in Korea, would try to capitalize on weak spots which might otherwise seem attainable at low cost. The U.N. army should be completely up-to-date. It should have access to such weapons as would be required to cope with the arsenal of any possible law-breaker.

The precedent for the establishment of such a force is Korea itself, with two significant differences. One is that the U.N. would not have to wait until the aggression was actually committed before recruiting a force of its own. The force would now be preventive rather than combative in purpose. The second difference is that the U.N. would no longer have to rely on the nation most vitally concerned to furnish the bulk of men and material. Surely the common cause of an enforceable peace is compelling enough for a fair and mandatory sharing of obligations. No question of good or bad faith is involved. Rather there must be a complete understanding by all nations concerning their world obligations and fixed responsibilities. No nation should have a valid basis for complaining that its own contribution is out of proportion to the total effort.

In the second phase of the timetable for interim security,

the plan for enforceable disarmament could come up. On the assumption that the U.N. force would have served its purpose—namely, to act as a shield behind which the U.N. could develop a sound basis for a workable peace—the next step would be control over national armaments. A bona fide request should be made of *all* nations. In return for participation in the plan for enforceable disarmament, each nation would have its security underwritten by the U.N., which by now would have substantial military authority, plus a call on immediate additional strength as needed.

The appeal of this proposal lies in the fact that the question of disarmament could now be considered inside an entirely different framework from the one that history had discredited. The new framework should have nothing to do with treaties or conventions—history is littered with the wreckage of such treaties and conventions. The new framework should be concerned with workable machinery, with enforcement measures; in short, with disarmament under law. No talk of disarmament makes sense, no proposed quotas for reduction of armaments is possible, unless the world's peoples could be confident that the success of any plan rests on something firmer than the good intentions of the agreeing parties.

In particular, a workable disarmament plan should call for control of all weapons adapted to mass destruction. Inspections and sanctions are mandatory to keep nations from engaging in such manufacture. Atomic energy, for example, should be developed under proper safeguards, with each nation participating as its own resources and industrial establishments would permit, and deriving benefits in proportion to the individual contribution to the over-all effort. This would not exclude other states from atomic benefits, particularly where health and economic development are concerned, but it would leave to those states with atomic-energy installations the primary rights of development and use for peaceful purposes. The U.N. inspectors would maintain careful safeguards against diversion of such facilities for military purposes. The U.N. would cease to manufacture atomic weapons once universal membership is achieved in the U.N. and the means for preventing war established.

The principal difference between this plan for control of atomic armaments and earlier proposals is that the U.N. would now be given powers against war itself. Under the Baruch Plan, for example, atomic disarmament was sought without any comparable machinery for dealing with the circumstances which might dictate the use of atomic weapons. No state under the proposed plan could justifiably argue that control of atomic energy was now being pursued in a vacuum, or that there was no agency strong enough to protect it against war and to ensure its rights.

The third phase of the work of the review conference might grow out of the previous two. Just as investing the U.N. with appropriate forces of its own is the precondition for any plan for enforceable disarmament, so the need to create a durable structure for carrying out disarmament would raise the question: What about the over-all form of the U.N. itself?

This form is inevitably related to its own powers and limitations. Law begins with the conquest of force. It moves through the agencies of justice and enforcement. It never allows potential violators to become stronger than the machinery to deal with violators. It is in the implementation of this idea that government takes shape. Whether that government is good or bad, whether it is a government in which all men are subject to the laws, including the leaders, or whether it is a government in which the laws serve the purposes of a few men or a man bent on capturing the state and its people—all these questions depend upon the wisdom and courage of the founders, the popular mandate behind them, and their ability to retain the confidence of the world's peoples.

It seems inescapable that the principles of federalism

would have to be seriously examined by a review conference if the United Nations is to possess adequate authority in the area of common security yet also be able to guarantee retention of internal sovereignty to the individual nations. Let us consider the alternatives.

First, a league. A league is a loose organization of states held together by treaty with the individual nations retaining ultimate authority even in armaments or other matters related to the common security. In view of the failures of leagues throughout history, including the United Nations and the League of Nations itself, it is to be hoped that the delegates would not tempt history further.

Next, a confederation. A confederation is a step beyond a league; that is to say, an attempt is made at a fairly organic relationship among the states and the obligations of all nations are generally fairly well defined. What a confederation lacks, however, is a structural basis for exacting obligations or for the adequate enforcement of its own rules. It lacks a common authority transcending national authority in those matters clearly concerned with common dangers and common needs.

Next, a strong central government. It is doubtful that the historic conditions exist at the moment for a strong central government of the world. Indeed, the easiest way to kill a centralized United Nations is to impose upon it functions and powers far beyond its capacity. A central government taking upon itself all the powers exercised by the individual nations—powers in the fields of taxation, currency, immigration, trade, economic development, mutual security and defense, general welfare, and so forth—would be dealing with such complexities and imponderables as could bring about its possible early collapse. Moreover, the differences in national institutions and cultures might create an almost insurmountable barrier for any government which attempted to maintain jurisdiction over the individual.

This leaves what is probably the soundest and safest approach of all to the revised structure of the U.N.; namely, a federation of limited but adequate powers. In such a federation, each nation would retain jurisdiction over its people and institutions in all matters except those clearly related to the common security and common development. There would be clear-cut distinctions between world jurisdiction and national jurisdiction, between the sovereignty that would be pooled in the federation and the sovereignty retained by the national states. The powers of a federated U.N. would be specifically confined to common needs and common dangers.

So far as jurisdiction over the individual is concerned, it would be restricted to those matters affecting the security of all peoples. The Nuremberg trials, it will be recalled, proceeded on the principle of individual responsibility and guilt for acts leading to war. What is needed now is exactly the same principle, except that this time the guilty parties should be apprehended in time to avert war rather than after the damage has been done and the dead counted.

Economic development, especially in the case of Asia and Africa, should be a signal opportunity for the federated U.N. It should be recognized, however, that many of the nations of Asia and Africa are just extricating themselves from a century or more of outside rule and that nothing should be done which could be regarded by those states as interference with their problems of internal development and control. Hence, it should be made clear that any requests for economic, technological, or scientific assistance to individual nations are to originate from the nations themselves. The greatest care should be taken to see that each development project would operate in a way consistent with each nation's own culture and institutions and that its own facilities with human resources would be fully utilized.

The U.N. already has within it many excellent agencies—

in the fields of world health, food, refugee problems, education, science, and so forth. But two things are in the way of their effective operation. The first is that these groups lack any real authority or the means of carrying out the necessary programs. The second is that the dominant energies and resources of most of the nations are being diverted to military purposes. The combination of authority and means could enable the special agencies of the U.N. to demonstrate high usefulness in improving the conditions of human existence.

These agencies, of course, would be directly responsible to, and established by, the legislative branch of the U.N.

Where would all this authority be lodged? In the General Assembly? The Security Council? It is doubtful that the big states would like to see important powers given to the General Assembly in its present form in view of the fact that they are on even footing with states with only a fraction of their own populations. Meanwhile, the Security Council, run by the big states, is bound by the unanimity principle. This means that no issue of consequence involving the major nations can be settled at present on the basis of strict adherence to law, for a major nation could negate the law through the veto.

Any attempt to redefine the authority of the General Assembly and Security Council, however, squarely opens up the entire question both of representation and of division of powers.

If a purely democratic basis were used for representation, then two or three populous nations might be able to dominate the voting. If a one-vote-for-one-state basis were used, then a few small states with perhaps an aggregate population of twenty million might be able to outvote nations with an aggregate population of 750,000,000 or more. This is perhaps the thorniest problem of all. There can be no authority without representation, but representation under existing circumstances seems impossible.

This dilemma may yield to the concept of *dual federalism* based on a regional approach inside the United Nations. Under this arrangement the General Assembly could be divided into its component regional parts, each of which would receive a total of one hundred votes or less, depending upon population, size, resources, and other vital factors. Each region would determine for itself the voting procedures for its own members in arriving at decisions concerning the vote that would be cast by the unit as a whole. A regional unit consisting of, say, ten members, two of which had a combined population larger than the combined total of the remaining eight members, might wish to give proportionate weight to the larger members in working out an equitable system of representation within itself. A regional unit might wish to split its hundred votes in the General Assembly, in order to reflect the mixed voting within itself on any question.

The advantage of the regional arrangement goes far beyond the possible solution it offers to the impasse of representation by population as against representation by nation. It recognizes a certain grouping of interests on the regional level—economic, cultural, political—and provides the means by which these natural interests could be protected and advanced.

The only questions on which the regional units need be called upon to vote as units in the General Assembly would be on matters involving the common security, or on relations of units to each other, or on the relations of members of one unit to members of another.

Dual federalism, then, is federalism of nations within regional units, and federalism of nations as members of regional units on the world level. The nation, the regional unit, and the federated U.N. would each exercise such sovereignty as was natural to it. The individual nations would have authority and jurisdiction in all matters pertaining to their own institutions and internal affairs. The regional units would have authority and jurisdiction in all matters pertaining to the regional needs and interests of its members. Finally, a federated U.N. would have authority and jurisdiction in those matters directly affecting the safety and vital needs of the world community.

As part of this general proposal, the Security Council might have to be reconstituted as an Executive Council. Its primary function would be to carry out the wishes and enforce the decisions of the General Assembly. The Executive Council would elect its own chairman and vice chairman, subject to ratification by the General Assembly. All the special agencies—disarmament, atomic controls, world health, food, economic development, refugees, and so forth—of the U.N. would come within the administration of the Council. The operating budget of the Council and its agencies would have to come before the General Assembly, which would have powers of appropriation and review.

The Executive Council, unlike its predecessor, the Security Council, would not be concerned with votes or vetoes within itself. It would not be a legislative agency but the principal enforcement arm of the United Nations. As such, it could make recommendations but it could not enact legislation or review it.

Judicial review of legislation enacted by the General Assembly, and of the enforcement activities of the Executive Council, would be vested in a World Court.

Perhaps the most comprehensive plan for strengthening the United Nations of any that have been advanced so far has come from Grenville Clark and Louis Sohn. Mr. Clark is a distinguished lawyer and expert in the field of international law. Mr. Sohn is professor of law at Harvard University. Their book, *World Peace Through World Law*,[1] is a detailed analysis of the problems involved in develop-

[1] Harvard University Press; revised edition, 1960.

ing the U.N. into a world organization capable of carrying out total disarmament and maintaining peace.

Their proposals embody a timetable for enactment and enforcement of Charter revisions, and the phasing out of world-wide, proportionate disarmament—concurrent with the building up of an international police force, fully safeguarded against misuse.

Here are the major changes they suggest in the structure and functions of the United Nations.

1. Membership in the U.N. must include every independent state in the world. Ratification of the revised U.N. Charter must be made by five-sixths of the nations, the ratifying nations to have a combined population of at least five-sixths of the total world population and to include *all* the twelve largest nations (Brazil, France, West Germany, India, Indonesia, Italy, Japan, Pakistan, Peoples' Republic of China, the U.K., the U.S.A., and the U.S.S.R.). The number of nonratifying nations must not exceed sixteen. Nonratifying nations shall nevertheless *be required to comply with the world-wide disarmament plan,* since even one small nation, possessed of a nuclear capability, can threaten the world.

2. Nations would not be forced to accept such affirmative obligations of U.N. membership as financial contributions, but *compliance with all provisions relating to disarmament is essential.* No nation, once having come into the U.N., could withdraw or be expelled.

3. Final responsibility for enforcement of the disarmament plan shall be vested in the General Assembly. It is recognized that the present system of unweighted representation (one vote for all nations, large or small) makes essential these changes:

(*a*) No nation shall have more than thirty Assembly delegates; (*b*) even the smallest nations shall have at least one. (The upper limit of thirty is recommended because weighted representation is not likely to be accepted by the smaller nations unless the differences between the majority of the nations and the largest nations are kept within moderate limits.)

4. The formula for weighted representation divides the ninety-nine nations (recognized in 1960 as independent states or likely to be by 1965) into six categories with representation as follows:

The 4 largest nations	30 representatives each, or			120
The 8 next largest nations ..	15	"	"	" 120
The 20 next largest nations ..	6	"	"	" 120
The 30 next largest nations ..	4	"	"	" 120
The 34 next largest nations ..	2	"	"	" 68
The 3 smallest nations	1	"	"	" 3
99 nations				551

representatives

Non-self-governing territories would be entitled to representation in proportion to their population on the same average basis as the peoples of the independent nations. (A bicameral legislature was ruled out, after considerable study.)

4. Within twenty-four years it is proposed that Assembly representatives be *chosen by popular elections in their countries*. During the interim, they are to be elected by their legislatures. Assembly decisions will be reached by majority vote, except on certain "important" and "special" questions.

These and other provisions for the General Assembly embody the concept of the U.N. as *far more* than a league of sovereign states represented by delegates *selected* by governments. It should be directly responsible to the peoples of the world. It is hoped that a spirit of world citizenship will develop, so that Assembly members would come to think of themselves as representing not only their countries but the entire world community.

5. To replace the present Security Council, an Executive

Council is proposed. Its seventeen members, *elected* for four-year terms by the General Assembly, would be responsible to and removable by the Assembly. China, India, the U.S.A., and the U.S.S.R. would have a representative in the Council at all times; four of the eight next largest nations would, in rotation, be entitled to membership with the proviso that two of these four members shall always be from European nations, the other two from nations outside Europe. The remaining nine members would be chosen by the Assembly from among the representatives of the other member nations and non-self-governing territories.

Except in special instances, a vote of any twelve members of the Council shall be required. (There would be no veto.) As the *executive arm* of the strengthened U.N., the Council would have a relation to the Assembly similar to that of the British Cabinet to the House of Commons. It would remain subordinate to the Assembly, which would have final authority on crucial decisions.

6. International disputes capable of settlement on legal principles would be referred by the Assembly to the International Court of Justice, which would have *compulsory* jurisdiction, *even if one of the parties should refuse to come before the Court*. The Court would also have authority to decide on questions relating to the interpretation of the revised Charter and to decide on constitutionality. Judges would be *elected* by the Assembly for life terms. Decisions would be enforced by economic sanctions or, in the last resort, action by the U.N. Peace Force.

7. A World Equity Tribunal, composed of fifteen persons elected by the Assembly for life, would take up international disputes not of an exclusively legal nature. Recommendations of the Tribunal, if not followed, would be relayed to the Assembly, where, by a three-quarters majority, they would become enforceable by the same means as a judgment of the International Court.

8. Disputes where *voluntary* settlement can be hoped for

would be referred to a World Conciliation Board. U.N. regional courts would prosecute individuals responsible for violation of disarmament provisions; a civil police force of the U.N. would aid in the detection and prosecution of such violators.

9. Following ratification of the revisions outlined above, the Assembly would convene to elect the Executive Council, which, in turn, would appoint an Inspection Commission to consist of five persons, none of whom would be a national of any of the twelve largest nations, and no two of whom would be a national of the same nation.

10. Under the provisions for the heavily inspected Arms Census, all nations would be required to supply full information on location and description of all military installations; manpower strength; organization, composition, and disposition of its military forces and all internal police forces; the location, kind, and quantity of all finished and unfinished arms and weapons (including nuclear, chemical, biological, etc.); the location, description, and rate of output of all facilities engaged in arms production and tools as well as those which have been engaged in such production during the past five years.

Records must be provided on the output and potential of all heavy industry plants which could be adapted to arms producton; on laboratories and other facilities engaged in work relating to weapons and the study of nuclear energy; on the amount and stage of processing of all raw materials within its territories which might be used in production of nuclear materials; on all special nuclear stockpiles and materials which have been made radioactive artificially; on mining activity which might enter into production of nuclear materials; on facilities utilizing special nuclear materials for research, industrial, commercial, or other nonmilitary purposes; on the number, kind, location, and stage of completion of all rockets, satellites, or spacecraft; on facilities engaged in production of same, and of tools for such production; on launching sites, etc.

U.N. inspectors would be vested with power necessary to verify information. In cases where nations fail to comply with the census requirements the disarmament plan would be suspended until noncompliance is ended. (Relatively short periods of suspension would be authorized by the Assembly—not more than six months at a time—to sustain pressure on recalcitrant nations.)

The limitation of six months upon any single postponement is intended to force renewed attention of the General Assembly at frequent intervals on any cause for postponement. The Assembly debates on the postponements would help focus world-wide attention on the reasons for and against proposed postponements. The result should be to discourage any delay in starting the actual process of disarmament, at the risk of arousing world opinion against the noncomplying nations.

11. With the completion and verification of the Arms Census, an Arms Truce would be called. At the same time, the Executive Council would issue a public announcement that the stage of actual disarmament would begin, bringing this historic fact to the attention of all the governments and peoples of the world. On that day a series of new obligations would become binding on all nations, and the arms truce would be supplemented by the progressive scaling down of all military forces, armaments, and facilities for arms production, *paralleled by the building up of a U.N. Peace Force.*

From the moment the Arms Truce is called, no nation in the world would be permitted to produce any military equipment and supplies or arms of any sort, or to engage in activities which might directly or indirectly sustain its military potential.

12. With respect to disarmament, a phased plan is pro-

posed, so that no nation need fear the consequences of compliance.

Gradual and *proportionate* elimination of military forces and arms is proposed to take place over a ten-year period at an annual 10 per cent reduction rate. It is evident that the plan can succeed only if it is carried out *simultaneously and proportionately*. Each nation shall scrap or disband *the same portion of the same capability at the same time*. The diminution of military strength would be equal for all nations. No nation would be expected to disarm by a larger percentage than others; no nation would be deprived of a main source of its strength while other nations still retain their principal sources of strength. Thus a nation strong in nuclear weapons would not be entirely deprived of them while other nations retain a large proportion of their preponderant land armies.

Similarly, a nation would not be asked to abandon its missiles while another is permitted to retain its bombers. For example: Under *uniform percentage reductions* (as opposed to *proportionate percentage reductions*) a nation might simply demobilize a large number of foot soldiers while leaving its air force unimpaired.

Each nation would be allowed to retain an internal police force, not to exceed two for each 1,000 of its population, and in no case to exceed 500,000. Light weapons would be rigidly restricted so as to prevent accumulation of armed strength and yet allow adequate internal security. Discarded arms and equipment would be put at the disposal of the U.N. Peace Force.

13. As the war-making capabilities of the nations decline and finally reach zero, a U.N. Peace Force comes into being. The possibility that the national internal police forces, although strictly limited and lightly armed, might constitute a serious threat to a neighboring country requires the existence of a well-disciplined and heavily armed world police.

To prevent domination of the Peace Force by any nation or group of nations, the number of nationals of any nation in its standing component would at no time exceed 3 per cent of the total strength of the Peace Force except in extreme emergencies. The Force would be composed of between 200,000 and 600,000 volunteer professionals. Units would be dispersed to avoid power concentrations, be highly mobile, and located in defensible positions, preferably on islands or peninsulas. None of them would be stationed in the larger countries.

14. Weapons capable of mass destruction (including biological, chemical, nuclear, etc.) would be prohibited to the Peace Force. Only upon declaration by the General Assembly that nuclear weapons (which might have been clandestinely hidden or produced) have been actually used against a nation, or threatened, would the U.N. Peace Force be permitted the use of its nuclear capability, which is to be held in the custody of a civilian agency at all times. (The use of nuclear weapons by the U.N. Peace Force in any other instance has been rejected as being no more consistent with the purposes of the Peace Force than the regular equipment of a city police force with weapons by which thousands of citizens could be killed in suppressing a riot.)

15. The U.N. Military Staff Committee would be under civilian control. Other specific precautions are outlined to subordinate the military direction to civilian authority and to prevent the perversion of the Peace Force into a tool of world domination.

16. Responsibility, it is hoped, for the accomplishment and maintenance of disarmament should be assumed as much as possible by the national governments. Hard provisions define and regulate the obligations of the nations to assure that all public and private organizations and individuals faithfully comply with the disarmament plan. An important element is the direct obligation of individuals and organizations to the U.N.

Elaborate provisions are made for inspection, including: special inspections without advance notice; authorization for inspectors to take temporary custody of any property discovered, the possession of which is prohibited; aerial surveys; rewards to persons supplying the Service with information relative to violations and safe asylum for informants and their families. A system of U.N. licensing of arms production would provide a practical and fair solution to the problem of internal security for each nation.

17. A U.N. Nuclear Authority is proposed. Designed to promote the fullest utilization of nuclear energy for peaceful purposes, it would also supplement the work of the U.N. Inspection Service by supervising certain critical stages in the production and distribution of special nuclear materials, both fusionable and fissionable.

The Authority would hold in temporary custody all special nuclear materials before their release to laboratories and facilities for scientific, industrial, commercial, and other nonmilitary purposes. It would, in addition to promoting as fully as possible the peaceful uses of nuclear materials, have the responsibility of providing the U.N. Peace Force with nuclear weapons when and if the Assembly so authorizes.

18. A U.N. Outer Space Agency is also proposed. Its purposes would be twofold: (1) to ensure that outer space is used for peaceful purposes *only,* and (2) to promote full exploration and exploitation of outer space for the common benefit of all mankind.

Its functions:

(*a*) To possess and operate its own rockets, satellites, and spacecraft, and to license the possession and operation of rockets, satellites, and spacecraft by nations, organizations, and individuals.

(*b*) To supervise the departure into space of both manned and unmanned craft.

(*c*) To promote international cooperation in the study of the problems of outer space.

(*d*) To conduct research on development of new rockets, satellites, and spacecraft.

(*e*) To supervise use of such equipment for peaceful purposes such as astronomy, meteorology, and communications.

(*f*) To prevent the use of outer space for military purposes and to keep other organs of the U.N. informed of any violation.

19. It may be advisable and possible to bring under the authority of the U.N. space exploration and space claims.

20. Since a main danger to world stability and peace is caused by vast economic disparities between countries, a World Development Authority would be created for the purpose of ameliorating these disparities by assisting the economic and social development of countries needing it—primarily through grants-in-aid and interest-free loans.

21. Such a world organization would require an estimated budget of $36 billion per annum. While this amount is less than one-half of the 1960-61 budget of the United States, it is considered impractical to rely on yearly assessments on the nations. To this end a *collaborative* revenue system is proposed whereby an over-all limit on the maximum amount of revenue to be raised in any given year would be set at 2 per cent of the gross world product. Annual amounts to be supplied by member nations would be calculated on the basis of that nation's estimated proportion of the estimated gross world product. This amount would be subject to a uniform "per capita deduction" of not less than 50 nor more than 90 per cent of the estimated per capita product of the ten member nations having the lowest per capita national product.

22. Despite all these powers, the U.N. would not enter the domain of internal authority. The proposed world con-

stitution is limited to those *minimum enumerated* powers necessary to prevent the nations from aggressing against one another. The world organization does not in any way deny or impair the right of man to privacy, dignity, well-being, and freedom—under law.

Whatever the specific plan may be for giving the United Nations the authority and machinery of world law, the main objections come from two broad groups. One group is opposed to any strengthening of the U.N. if there is any danger that not all nations would accept. The other group is opposed to a federated U.N. if all nations *were* given the opportunity to accept.

In a sense, both groups have much in common. Neither recognizes the essential nature and purpose of government under law. Federal government is not organized for the purpose of distributing favors for those who accept membership. Nor is its primary purpose the imposition of penalties for those who fail to accept.

The purpose of federal government is to provide a rational, just, and workable method for the definition and enforcement of valid obligations among nations in the interests of common safety. The question of desirability of membership comes up only if the organization is a league or a confederation. Lacking authority of its own, a league or confederation could be dominated by recalcitrant or obstructive members. But federation is not without means and resources of its own to deal with obstructive members. Indeed, its very reason for being is that it assumes that there will always be natural or unnatural controversy among its members and that its main function is to keep such controversy from erupting in war.

Federalists contend that the widest possible latitude should be given to all nations for the fullest possible consideration of membership and that no fixed deadline be set for acceptance. In the event that some nations would wish to see the federated U.N. in action over a period of time before deciding finally on the advantages or disadvantages of membership, such protracted consideration should not be regarded by the others necessarily as being unfriendly.

To repeat: What needs to be created is not an exclusive club dispensing privileges but an organization of the nations exacting obligations. The greater the menace to the peace a nation might be, the greater the need to have that nation within a workable system of security. The established method of dealing with a law-breaker is not to exempt him from the laws but to use the full machinery of the law to keep him within reach.

The main problem, however, is not to devise means to keep some nations out but to get them all to come in. Related to this is the need to recognize that if the free world waits too long to propose federation it might be confronted by a totalitarian bloc enjoying a majority which would attempt to set up a world government of its own.

Such a world government would not be federal in form. It would not rest upon principles of justice; it would not provide for equitable representation; it would not be one which, in the final analysis, would look for its ultimate power to the world's peoples. The source of its authority would be force.

A federal government, however, built on concepts of world justice could resolve at least that aspect of the danger to world peace resulting from competitive insecurity.

World federation will not by itself solve all the world's problems. But it may release resources to man for higher ends—the pursuit of justice and a purposeful life. And if nothing else is achieved, at least for the first time in history the human community would have its own voice.

XI. *What About Russia?*

LIKE the chant of a Greek chorus rising to a crescendo, one question repeats itself at every point along the way in the development of the argument for control over power in the modern world. What about Russia? How do we get the Soviet Union to agree to enforceable control over nuclear weapons—not just the testing of the weapons but the manufacture and even disposition of the weapons? How do we get the Soviet to agree to the measures necessary to do away with world anarchy? How do we get the Soviet to agree to the conversion of the United Nations into a world authority with adequate powers—powers reaching down to the individual in those matters concerned with the common security of the world's peoples?

In short, aren't all the warnings about the nature of nuclear war and the exhortations about need of genuine peace academic unless the major nations agree to do the things that are essential to create such a peace? And what indications are there that the Soviet Union would be willing to agree to such far-reaching measures, especially those that call for a modification of her sovereignty? If the communist world believes that war is probable purely in terms of the dynamics of the power struggle, then how could it have confidence in measures that seek to avert war? In the context of missile-nuclear warfare, couldn't this dictate the need to hit first?

There are yet other questions. Isn't world communism bent on world conquest? If so, isn't it only a matter of time before this ideological drive leads to a major war? Revolutions have a way of throwing out dangerous sparks. The spread of communist ideologies to Africa and Latin America is certain to raise grave security questions for the United States, Great Britain, and France. The world balance of power contest involves not just bombs and missiles and troops but economic and political change in the world.

Such being the case, how is it possible to talk seriously about the prospects of an enduring peace? Is there any reason to suppose that the Soviet Union would set aside her ideological aims in favor of a structured peace?

Finally, what about a possible conflict between Marxist dogma and the requirements of world peace? Karl Marx believed that war was inherent in the nature of capitalism. He saw in *laissez-faire* economics a cycle that led to war. The industrial establishment would have to produce to make profits. In the absence of controls over production, the race for profits would lead to over-production. The men who toiled at the machines would receive wages too low to permit them to buy the things they produced. This led to a struggle for control of overseas markets and for imperialistic supremacy. This would create a need for the production of war goods. The economy would become increasingly dependent on armaments as a means of keeping it in full operation. The combination of struggle for world markets and the militarism that went along with the armaments race would lead to war by accident or design.

To the extent that this theory is accepted as a valid one by Soviet leaders, how does it affect the possibilities of peace?

Questions such as these are asked not solely by those who are chemically opposed to anything involving the

Soviet Union in particular and world communism in general. They are asked by many people who accept the need to explore agreements with the Soviet Union but who are nonetheless pessimistic about the prospects that such agreements can be reached or will work even if reached. They are willing to try; but they entertain no solid hopes for success.

These questions, and the problems they pose, must be considered on two different levels. One is the national level, in which the actions of the Soviet Union are dictated by the traditional characteristics of national fears and ambitions. The other is the ideological level, in which the actions of the Soviet Union are related to her Marxist role in world affairs as the Soviet leaders interpret it.

Each of these levels has its own set of requirements. Each calls for specific policies. Sometimes the policies in the national level are in conflict with the ideological one. Sometimes they are in complete accord. Generally, they interact. But always, they are separate in their origins.

It becomes important, therefore, to consider the Soviet Union's relationship to world peace according to the two dominant forces that figure in its policy.

As a nation, the Soviet Union is first of all a full sovereign state, affected by all the historical considerations that traditionally govern the jockeying for power and security in the world arena. The quest for alliances or balance-of-power or supremacy of one sort or another is a basic characteristic of the sovereign state. Ever since human society arranged itself in groups, the pattern has remained substantially the same.

Nations exhibit all the variable characteristics of people. Some have been content with modest size and achievements. Others have been acquisitive and insatiable. Some have been eager only to live quietly and unobtrusively. Others have been noisy and obnoxious. Some have sought only self-sufficiency. Others have been predatory, ruthless, aggressive.

Despite this range of behavior, one historic fact clearly emerges. The larger a nation, the more certain it is to get involved in traffic problems with other large nations. It seeks economic power and prosperity and, like an individual, it tries to get the best bargains in its dealings with others. But, unlike the individual, it is not restrained by properly constituted agencies of law in the way it goes about advancing its interests. And when those interests come into conflict with the interests of others, the absence of a tribunal with compulsory jurisdiction adds to the natural determination of a nation to stand its ground or assert its position.

Similarly, the pursuit of security is a precarious and volatile enterprise. The small nation or even the large unarmed one has had no protection against the acquisitive, aggressive nation. This has led to treaty arrangements, coalitions, balance-of-power attempts, large armaments. Here, too, the absence of a code backed by enforcement agencies has not protected the peace-loving state against aggression. Neither has the armed but non-aggressive large state been protected against the tensions of insecurity.

As a nation, therefore, the Soviet Union has made decisions and taken action that would have been made and taken quite apart from its underlying ideology or political philosophy. A large part of the foreign policy of the Soviet Union, in fact, has come forward in a straight line from the policy under Czarist Russia. The need for a military cushion in Central Europe; the fear of Germany; the determination to have outlets on the Baltic and Black Sea; the apprehension over the encroaching population pressure from China—all these were in evidence long before the Communist Revolution. The existence of a world ideology may have modified or enhanced some of the purposes or objectives or the way in which they are met, but the sovereign concerns are substantially what they have been all along.

The fact that the Soviet Union has invoked the veto in the United Nations Security Council so frequently may be less a reflection of its ideology than of its sovereignty. It was the United States, and not the Soviet Union, that proposed the veto for the U.N. Security Council. This was no more a projection of the democratic political philosophy of the United States than the frequent use of the veto by the Soviet Union was a projection of Marxian dogma. In both cases, the right of ultimate national decision was being upheld.

It is also true that neither the Soviet Union nor the United States nor any of the other major nations have come forward to propose an abolition of the veto as part of a system of compulsory jurisdiction inside a revamped United Nations. All the large nations have resisted the need to subordinate their sovereignty to a world organization, or even to consider what the circumstances would be that would enable them to have confidence in the ability of a world organization to create just standards of national behavior and justly to enforce them.

On the national level, therefore, the questions concerning the willingness of the Soviet Union to accept a structured peace are valid ones, but they apply with perhaps equal cogency to all the major nations. This doesn't make the task any easier, but it at least helps to identify the main problem. If a structured peace is to become a reality, the fallacies and dangers of unfettered national sovereignty will have to be met by many nations and not just by one or two.

Since the sovereign state, whatever its ideology, will be reluctant to modify itself, it becomes essential for peoples to help shape the national decisions. Obviously, this is much more likely in countries enjoying free expression of public opinion than in those that do not. Even so, no nation can insulate itself entirely from the ferment of world opinion. No nation, however efficient its sound-proofing mechanism, can silence all the reverberations of a world debate on the requirements of human survival. Nothing is more mysterious in human affairs than the penetrating power of great ideas.

In any event, the great debate will have to proceed in three stages. The first occurs through citizen initiative inside those nations where important debate is possible. The aim is to persuade the national governments to bring the question of world law and a structured peace before the U.N. The second great stage of the debate occurs inside the United Nations, where the whole question of meaningful survival is related to the adequacy of the U.N. itself. The third stage of the debate is what happens in all countries, whatever the form of their government, when the impact of a great idea directed to a structured peace for the entire human community makes itself felt.

A consensus in favor of a governed world is not going to take place overnight. But everything begins with advocacy and debate. Just in the process of arguing the great ideas, a new context for the human situation begins to emerge.

In this new context, the Soviet Union will not be called upon to make any concessions that all the others will not have to make.

If the Soviet Union is basically motivated by considerations of security, then only a world organization with adequate powers to underwrite the common safety and the independence of all nations will be able to provide such security.

If the Soviet Union believes in disarmament, then only a strong United Nations will be able to bring it about, and, what is more important, be able to enforce it.

Neither the Soviet Union nor anyone else will be expected to give up its national identity, its cultural pattern, or its political philosophy. Indeed, its independence will be assured by the U.N.

What the Soviet Union *will* have to give up—as will all the others—is the ability to wage nuclear war and surprise attack. Moreover, it will have to submit to the jurisdiction of a world society on those matters concerning the common safety and welfare of the human commonwealth.

Since the alternative is likely to be no world at all—for the Soviet Union or anyone else—there is a reasonable prospect that the proposal will be seriously considered.

This leaves unanswered so far the question of the Soviet Union as an ideology. What is there in the ideology of communism that may interfere with the need for communist nations to be joined with opposing economies and ideologies inside a structured world organization with binding obligations?

The first fact that has to be considered is that the history of the Soviet Union since its revolution has seen many major changes. Far from being rigid in its basic positions, the Soviet has made not just tactical shifts in its position but fundamental alterations in ideology and policy.

Very early in its history, for example, Lenin interpreted Marx in a way that was to change profoundly the direction of the Soviet Union. He declared that it was incorrect to believe—as many Marxist scholars had believed—that it was essential to have a world socialist revolution before socialism could succeed in any one country.

A series of other profound changes in the Soviet Union occurred after the death of Josef Stalin. With each shift in the top command, ideological and political changes of varying degrees of importance took place.

One of the most fundamental of these changes occurred in the early period of Nikita Khrushchev's Chairmanship of the Communist Party. Re-interpreting Karl Marx, Mr. Khrushchev declared it was possible to seek and achieve peaceful relations with capitalist nations. It was not necessarily true, according to the new interpretation, that war was inherent in the nature of capitalism. Karl Marx, Mr. Khrushchev declared, had no way of anticipating the great changes that were to take place in the twentieth century. He could not foresee the nature of new weapons. Moreover, there were powerful new developments inside the capitalist nations themselves that were unanticipated.

This change in ideology may have been related to the need to forestall or prevent a war with the West both in view of the annihilating character of the new weapons and the emergence of another powerful communist nation with which the long-term *national* interests of the Soviet Union might be in conflict. This latter fact was not foreseen by Marx.

Czarist Russia was never comfortable about large population masses on its borders, especially in Asia. In the nineteenth century and early twentieth century, Russia made several attempts to dominate the Asian complex. What it feared was that its lands might become the spillway for the surplus population of Asia in general and China in particular. It looked ahead and foresaw a situation in which China, whatever the complexion of its government or political philosophy, would become expansionist because of the sheer massed weight of numbers.

If the fact of population pressure from the East was a valid concern for Russia in the nineteenth century, it carries even greater weight in the latter half of the twentieth century. By the end of the century, the population of China will be in excess of one billion, two hundred million people. China has been restoring millions of acres of eroded land to productivity, and she has been scoring impressive gains in the agricultural yield in existing farmland. But the rate of population increase has been moving faster than the increase in the food supply.

Southeast Asia is already overcrowded; it is doubtful whether the population spillover would be in that direction. The heartland of Siberia is one of the few Asian areas rich enough to sustain a large population influx.

In any event, the emergence of two national goliaths both adhering to communist ideology but impelled by natural forces in different directions was not anticipated by Karl Marx. The Soviet ideological leaders have therefore interpreted Marx's ideas about world socialist unity in the light of their own national requirements.

In short, where ideological adherence and national purpose come into conflict, national purpose tends to prevail.

Another example of this can be observed on the economic level.

The U.S.S.R., like the United States, measures the strength of its economic system by its productivity. In those cases where productivity, strictly following Marxist orthodoxy, has not been as high as it should be, the orthodoxy is modified. The Soviet economy has developed into a blend between socialization at the level of public service and national capitalism at the level of production. The state is the investor and entrepreneur; it seeks maximum productivity and uses capital as the medium of exchange by which people are paid for producing and by which the goods are sold.

The need to be productive has resulted in incentives for labor. And the existence of incentives has resulted in adoption of certain capitalistic procedures, albeit under state auspices. Laborers in many instances are paid on a piecework basis, with substantial bonuses where quotas have been met or surpassed.

In agriculture, orthodox ideological measures led to inadequate productivity. Hence the orthodoxy was severely modified. Farmers were permitted to own small tracts of their own, the yield from which they could use or sell as they wished. They still had to work the land that was collectively owned. But the rewards were high for those who exceeded the quotas. Extra payments and cash bonuses were given to the especially productive. This in turn resulted in some discrepancies in living standards and purchasing power.

A number of features in the Soviet economy would not conform to classical Marxist ideology; but the point is that the ideology has been made flexible enough to embrace what the Soviet leaders considered to be a larger purpose.

The same is probably true on the international level in the making of peace.

There is scope neither for ideological fulfillment nor national purpose in nuclear suicide. It therefore becomes as mandatory for the Soviet Union as it is for everyone else to dispose of the danger of war and proceed with its objectives by other means.

Obviously, the Soviet Union would like to have the terms of peace serve its long-range purposes. But it is to her own self-interest to have a durable peace even if it confers no special advantage.

The same is true of the United States and every nation on earth. A structured peace—effective law through a revamped United Nations—will not of itself put an end to political or economic or ideological competition in the world. It will not create compatibility where none now exists. What it can do is to make the world safe for its diversity and clear the stage for non-violent competition among the great forces of the world.

Even if a governed world can be devised, it will not represent the ultimate in human aspiration and achievement. The problem of more people than the world can creatively sustain—a problem that will press heavier with each passing year; the problem of scarcity in most areas and superabundance in a few; the problem of unresolved geographic boundaries and contested territories; the problem of freedom for those countries still under outside rule; the problem of refugees; the problem of mandated territories; the problem of minorities; the problem of world health—all these problems and many more will continue, some of them in intensified form, even though a governed world can be brought into being.

The only difference will be that for the first time the world's peoples will have available to them the rational means for dealing with basic issues and tensions among nations. Fixed limits will be set to the character of the competition among conflicting ideologies. Most significantly, the preponderance of the world's energies will be released for an attack on its basic needs—food, health, education.

In any event, not until proposals for a governed world are put before the United Nations with full seriousness of purpose does the question—what about Russia?—become totally relevant. And even though the initial response may be negative, the fact of such proposals constitutes a vital rallying ground in themselves. For they represent the greatest cause on earth—the cause of human society made safe for itself.

And the value of the response will be represented not just by what one or more nations will say in opposition but by what the preponderance of the world's peoples will say. The nature of the total response can create a new mood in the world. And out of this new mood vital new realities can be fashioned.

For it is not what the Americans can do by themselves, or what the Russians can do by themselves, that will determine the shape or the splendor of their societies. Their destinies will be determined by their mutual ability to create and sustain a *structured* peace. If they should fail in this enterprise, then all their other enterprises—the giant turbines, hydroelectric power installations, mass-assembly belts, housing projects, jet planes, rockets, supermarkets, superhighways, or ballet theaters—all these will serve only as monuments to the scientific genius and political imbecility of a race of extinct warriors.

XII. *The Habit of Violence*

PEACE is retarded not solely by the absence of a world organization capable of taming and regulating the rational societies.

Peace can be retarded by human habits and conditionings.

There is the habit of violence. There is also an environmental conditioning that tends to impede the natural desire in people to make commitments to people far away they may never know.

Begin with violence. The causative range runs all the way from childhood experiences to the proclamations of nations.

In a phrase, all now agree that violence in a nuclear age is unthinkable. But what is thinkable? And who is doing the thinking? What great alternatives to violence are being fashioned? What great new ideas are being advanced for eliminating violence while safeguarding human values?

The same heads of state who have declared that nuclear war is unthinkable do not hesitate to think in nuclear terms. On one hand, they agree that nuclear war is too terrible to become a reality. Yet it is in the name of realism that they devise policies based on nuclear force. Each side is trying to convince the other that it wouldn't have the slightest hesitation to fight a nuclear war that both have declared to be out of the question. A strange game is being played in which ultimatums are issued in the name of nuclear force, and would result in mutual suicide. Both sides have acknowledged this probability, yet each seems to feel the success of its own policy depends on its ability to threaten the other with joint suicide. In effect, each assumes that the other places a higher value on staying alive. To paraphrase Emerson, violence is in the saddle and is riding man.

The old forms of preparedness by which a nation pursues security no longer work. We are obligated, therefore, to embark on a new form of preparedness. It is the kind of preparedness which begins by taking seriously the need to look beyond violence. This may well be the most difficult undertaking in human history.

Violence has become a seemingly normal part of routine living. Almost from the moment a child is old enough to observe or talk, violence is glamorized for him and made part of his emotional diet. His earliest games have to do with violence or the instruments of violence. Year in and out, the biggest sellers in toys are guns or other make-believe weapons. Even religion has been made to glorify violence. Sunday School in too many cases has become less an adventure in the higher reaches of the human spirit than a grandstand seat in an arena of interminable warfare. There is little compassion for slain people when they happen to be on the other side. Not much is said about the tragedy of human conflict; the battle is the thing. Even the Deity is vested with certain violent and vindictive moods; He is not above stoning people when they displease Him, and innocent children are punished for the sins of remote ancestors. There is a hard wall of separation between the sublime and non-violent ethics of the Sermon on the Mount and their application in everyday life. It is as though it were more important to belong than it is to believe.

Wherever we turn we find reflections of this casual approach to violence. It is one thing to kill animals for food or for the protection of crops. It is another thing to kill them for the fun of it. And numberless persons take part in this exercise out of sheer enjoyment. Arguments are advanced in justification; i.e., some animals might multiply excessively and become a drain on the land. But problems such as these can be routinely handled if they become serious enough. The heart of the matter is that some people like to cause injury or death to living things. And many of those who do not are indifferent to those who do.

Some of our sports appeal directly to the fascination with violence. A great deal is said about the art of boxing but the prizefight promoters who make the matches are on the constant lookout not for boxers but for killers. They know that it is the killer who attracts the crowds. No large crowd was ever brought screaming to its feet by two boxers who parried each other's blows. The crowd comes to life when hard-driving smashes to a man's heart or his head cause him to stare blankly and then go down. When people say they have seen a good fight they mean they have seen someone badly hurt. Now and then a man is beaten to death in the ring; his brain is unable to withstand repeated hammering. People shake their heads sadly and either call it an accident or say it's all in the game. In any case, authorized murder has taken place in full view of thousands of people.

Violence is not confined to the man in the fight arena or to the man with a gun in the field. It is an important staple in the regular entertainment diet. The large majority of films or television productions hold violence to be almost as essential as the camera itself. Thus, the slightest disagreement between two men in a play is accompanied by the explosion of a fist in a human face. This is as routine as opening an umbrella in the rain. There is little respect in our entertainment for the fragility of human life.

The natural reactions of the individual against violence are being blunted. He is being desensitized by living history. He is developing new reflexes and new responses that tend to slow up the moral imagination and relieve him of essential indignation over impersonal hurt. He is becoming casual about brutality. He makes his adjustments to the commonplace, and nothing is more commonplace in our age than the ease with which life can be smashed or shattered. The range of the violence sweeps from the personal to the impersonal, from the amusements of the crowd to the policies of nations. It is in the air, quite literally. It has lost the sting of surprise. We have made our peace with violence.

No idea could be more untrue than that there is no connection between what is happening in the world and the behavior of the individual. Society transfers its apprehensions or its hopes, its fatigues or its vitality, its ennui or its dreams, its sickness or its spirituality, to the people who are part of it. Can the individual be expected to retain the purity of his responses, particularly a sensitivity to the fragility of life, when society itself seems to measure its worth in terms of its ability to create and possess instruments of violence that could expunge civilization as easily as it once took to destroy a village? Does it have no effect on an individual to live in an age that has already known two world wars; that has seen hundreds of cities ripped apart by TNT tumbling down from the heavens; that has witnessed whole nations stolen or destroyed; that has seen millions of people exterminated in gas chambers or other mass means; that has seen governments compete with one another to make weapons which, even in the testing, have put death in the air?

The individual takes on the habits of his society. He is one cell of a larger living organism. When the total organism becomes ill or irrational, the individual cell is affected by the deviations and often reflects them.

The desensitization of twentieth-century man is more

than a danger to the common safety. It represents the loss or impairment of the noblest faculty of human life—the ability to be aware both of suffering and of beauty; the ability to share sorrow and to create hope; the ability to think and to respond beyond one's wants. There are some things we have no right ever to get used to. One of these most certainly is brutality. The other is the irrational. Both brutality and the irrational have now come together and are moving toward a dominant pattern. If the pattern is to be resisted and changed, a special effort must be made. A very special effort.

The fact that public issues are not made of these things is significant in itself. For the casualness with which violence is treated and accepted may make it difficult for us to think today in totally different terms, even though our lives may now depend on our ability to do so. There is a universal chorus behind the proposition, to repeat, that violence in a nuclear age is unthinkable. But it is not enough merely to itemize the unthinkables in order to produce sanity and safety. It becomes important to replace the unthinkables with the workables.

Equal in importance, perhaps, to the problem represented by the habit of violence is the sense of disconnectedness between man and man.

The need to be needed is a basic requirement for human emotional health. The inability to satisfy this need fully is one of the prime facts of life in the modern world. Except in a disaster or emergency, there is an inadequate outlet for the natural longing of a human being to share fully and freely. We have become masters of the impersonal and the inanimate. Our energy and even our emotions have gone into things; the things serve us but come between us, changing the relationship of man to man. And the things take on an authority that men accept without protest.

The impersonality is epidemic. It is almost as though we feared direct contact, almost as though the soul of man had become septic.

If a man becomes ill he hardly hangs up his hat in the doctor's office before he is placed in front of a whole battery of machines and testing devices. The traveled road is not between the mind of the diagnostician and the heart of the patient, but between the clinic and the laboratory. There comes to mind Castiglione's admonition that the post of honor for the doctor is at the bedside of his patient.

If a man submits himself for a job he is seen not as a personality but as a fit subject for various tests which presumably have more to do with ascertaining his worth than the human responses which may figure largely in the work he is called upon to do.

If a man builds a house he no longer participates in a wonderful joint enterprise with neighbors, but in a juggling contest with figures, and he may not see his neighbors from one year to the next. The house itself may be shiny and functional, but not a thing is known about the people who made it.

If a man wishes to help needy people he generally does it not on a man-to-man basis but through an agency; and his contribution becomes a statistic rather than a strand in a lifeline thrown out to a recognizable being.

Even current philosophies give weight to the notion that people as people are not really essential to each other. Most existentialists dislike to be taxed with the charge that their doctrine is essentially negative, but the fact remains that a strong branch of their philosophy is based on the absoluteness of the separation between man and man. It holds that man is chained to his alone-ness, that there is no way for him—even in the hour of his greatest need—to penetrate beyond the barrier of self. In this sense, of course, Existentialism is a modern echo of the Egyptian philosophy of the individual as set down by Schiller: "I am that which is. I am all, what is, what was, what will be. No man has lifted my veil. He is only and solely for himself . . ."

But man is more than the shadow of his substance, more than a self-contained and self-sealing entity. He comes to life in others and is affected by their hurts or their needs or their moral splendor. When he denies this, no matter how slick the apparatus of sophistication behind the denial may be, he hammers at the essence of his own being.

An ice age can come about inside man through a lowering of the temperature of human response. As against this, there is always the possibility that men will come to see their commitment to each other as the basic energy and power of their civilization.

XIII. *Visit to the Atomic City*

THE best-run city in the United States is probably Los Alamos, the fast-growing atomic metropolis sprung up on a mountain shelf in New Mexico. A visitor isn't inside the city very long before he is aware of the cleanness of the place, the excellence of the roads, the superb school and hospital facilities, the housing arrangements, and, in general, the evidence of a successfully planned city. It is a closed city, however, for it is one of the headquarters concerned with making the nuclear explosives that can expunge in a fraction of a second some of the vast aggregations of concrete, wood, and people that make up the units of twentieth-century civilization.

At Los Alamos more is known about the highly organized science of demolition than has ever been learned at any place in human history. This is where the experts pool their knowledge and do the laboratory and engineering work that go into the building of the big bombs. It is the experts' job to stay ahead in the atomic armaments race, which means that they must strive for constant progress. There is a widely held view that the security of the nation depends on the ability of the laboratories to devise atomic improvements and then embody them in far more destructive units than have been made previously. The possible flaw in this theory is that only a certain number of the big bombs may be needed to achieve a desired total result, especially if they are used under circumstances which may make retaliation difficult or academic.

As a visitor, I wasn't privileged to see what was going on inside the big concrete sheds. But I did get some idea of the vast scope of the project and the meticulous organization that went into it. I was impressed with the visible evidence of a city dedicated to science that was itself operated so scientifically. The one thing I kept wondering about, however, was why there were no comparable cities anywhere in the world devoted to the spirit of man and the cause of peace. The danger of Los Alamos was represented not so much by the things that came out of it as by the fact that there was a monstrous lack of something to balance it on the outside. Los Alamos was a symbol of the growing one-sidedness of modern man. Where were the big ideas equal to the challenge of the big bombs? Where was the equivalent scientific thought and research on how to make the big bombs unnecessary?

By far the most interesting sidelight of the trip to Los Alamos was a visit to the electronic brain. The business of dealing with nuclear fission involves calculations far beyond the limited ability of mere mortals—taking the time factor into account, of course. The electronic brain is not prepossessing in appearance. It couldn't have been more than seven feet high and three feet thick. Most of the innards are visible through the grillwork. I saw a veritable fairyland of tubes of all sizes lighted with varying degrees of brightness. Bulbs flash off and on and the brain utters clicking sounds not unlike an energetic pinball machine giving someone a good run for his money.

Man communicates with this superior intellect by typing his problem on a card, where punched holes take the place of words. Incidentally, the machine has a vocabulary of somewhat more than one thousand words, enough for its purposes. The cards are fed into one side of the machine with a resultant intensification of clicking sounds and blinking of lights, as though the brain is mumbling to itself while it counts on its electronic frontal lobes. Some problems are more difficult than others and the brain requires more time to figure them out. On an average problem, though, the brain is fairly prompt, ascertaining the precise question and then providing an answer within a matter of minutes. The answer comes out on the far end of the machine in the same form the question went in: a punched card that has to be translated back into a reply intelligible to a human brain.

Atop the cabinet, in the place of honor, are the sealed boxes where the memory centers of the electronic brain are located. For all its computing skills, the brain has an astonishingly short memory. On most problems it can retain its own answers for only twenty-four hours. However, this is much better than the earlier species, in which the memory functioned for only a fraction of that time. Highly differentiated electronic tubes account for the improvement, but the makers of the brain are not satisfied with memory performance that doesn't extend much beyond a single day, and they aim to develop the brain even further.

The big shortcoming of the brain, of course, is that it doesn't know the first thing about creating alternatives and then choosing between them. It registers an absolute blank on the major part of any question; namely, what to do with an answer after it is found. It can calculate the precise heat registered in the heart of a nuclear explosion, but it knows absolutely nothing about the heart of a man. It can't analyze human experience and come up with an answer based on history itself, nor can it prescribe a course of action that would keep its masters free of the cosmic heats and radioactivity it measures so beautifully. In short, the brain has no advice to offer about enlarging human freedom under enforceable peace and justice. It doesn't know beans about making moral judgments.

The fact that the human brain is still superior to its electronic child in these respects should be reassuring, but it isn't. The big test of our time isn't involved with astronomical calculations. It involves choice, it involves decision, it involves access to history, it involves moral judgments.

The disturbing thought I had on leaving the atomic headquarters of Los Alamos was that we may be a little premature in lording it over the electronic brain because of its failure to understand the mechanism of decision. The uniqueness of the human mind must be demonstrated, rather than merely assumed, if the uniqueness of man himself is to be made real.

On my way back from Los Alamos, I got to musing about electronic brains. It could answer many questions that were ostensibly beyond human intelligence—or at least it could provide answers in short order that the human mind could furnish only after many hours or even days of sustained effort. Why shouldn't it be possible to construct an electronic brain that could furnish answers based on human historical experience with war and peace?

Then musings led me to write a fantasy in the form of a letter from a hypothetical scientist explaining how such a brain might operate:

"There is no doubt," the letter says, "that electronic thinking machines can be helpful in answering questions of a non-mathematical nature. We have now devised a brain that knows how to choose and to make decisions. You might say it offers us electronic wisdom.

"The significance of our research, we believe, should be apparent to all those in the social studies, for the electronic brain is now able to furnish accurate answers in the fields of history, economics, and political science.

"Our electronic brain operates on the basis of mathematical equations, though its capacity to deal with variables and unknowns is increased prodigiously over the older models. The job we give the machine to do is to make selections from among possible answers based on a wide variety of historical factors. It examines various approaches to certain problems and then gives each a comparative rating.

"Let me give you a specific example. One of our earliest experiments involved taxation. This was our hypothetical problem: A government wishes to raise ten million dollars in additional taxation. Four different plans are drawn up. Which is best? We collect and put down on cards all the pertinent factual data concerning previous experience—ratio of cost of collection to actual tax receipts, delinquency percentage, relationship to the national economy, effect on spending or saving, etc. All these factors involve actual figures. The accurate evaluation of these countless figures would require weeks of effort for even the most competent human mind. The machine can make instantaneous correlations; it is not conditioned by emotional or political factors.

"In this particular case the electronic brain gave us a rating on each of the proposed plans and selected a tax that would impose a minimum of hardship with a maximum of revenue.

"Now we have reason to believe that it should be possible to extend the brain's memory and vocabulary indefinitely. The implications of this are far-reaching. What it means is that a thinking mechanism exists which not only can calculate far beyond human ability but which possesses and utilizes far more wisdom than is within the range of human capacity. Consider the implications of this on the affairs of government and business. Indeed, it will affect morals, philosophy, education, economics—even our spiritual life. It will be able to penetrate the veil of cosmic mysteries. It may expose great historical fallacies, just as it may have some vast but harsh truths to reveal about man himself.

"But my primary purpose is to tell you about our forthcoming report on the major experiments with the new-style electronic brain. Encouraged with our success on such problems as taxation, we decided to take a big jump and put to the machine the number one problem before the world's people today—the problem of peace.

"We enlisted the full-time efforts of nine historians from universities in Europe and Asia. The historians built up an enormous card file of historical data pertinent to war and peace. We worked out a system whereby numerical values were assigned to different groupings of historical information.

"In all, almost 63,000 cards were thus compiled on man's experiences in trying to avert war. Each card contained factual data for a dozen or more equations. Thus, the electronic brain was called upon to correlate and test some 780,000 sets of facts, with some 1,654,000,000 possible combinations of relevant factors that would go into any study on how to achieve lasting peace. This, clearly, was beyond individual human intelligence. We estimated that the correlation of these factors alone would require sixty men working for a period of not less than fifteen years.

"I am oversimplifying for purposes of clarity. In essence, what we did was to give the electronic brain the principal methods used to preserve peace in the past—treaties, coalitions, balance-of-power arrangements, organic union, etc. Each of these methods was tested against every possible historical situation or combination of circumstances.

"When, finally, all this data was introduced into the brain, we waited anxiously and apprehensively for the result. We didn't even know whether the experiment would work. Many of us entertained serious doubts about our experiment. We had tried to be as scientific as possible in preparing the data, and we had cross-checked our numerical assignments. But the possibility for human error in drawing up these numerical assignments was not inconsiderable.

"In any event, the day for the big test arrived. The 63,000 cards were fed into the machine in proper sequence at the rate of 240 a minute. Within nineteen minutes after the last card was introduced, the electronic brain began to return its answers.

"The machine had digested the information, made its incredibly difficult correlations and evaluations, and was now supplying the answers.

"The machine's answers can be divided into three categories. First, a collation of information about past wars. Second, an estimate of the cost in life and property of an atomic war. Third, an evaluation of previous approaches to peace, together with a recommended course of action for averting another war.

"First: Information about previous wars.

"1. Since 3600 B.C. there have been only 292 years of peace. The records list 14,513 wars of minor and major character.

"2. Approximately 1,240,000,000 human beings have been killed by war or the diseases produced by war. (This would mean one out of every four persons who have lived since 3600 B.C. has been a war casualty.)

"3. Total cost of damage produced by the world's wars is approximately \$500,000,000,000,000,000,000. (This would be enough to run a band of gold 100 miles wide, thirty feet thick, around the circumference of the globe.)

"Second: Grouping of facts concerning the nature of an atomic war. The most important single fact to emerge from the evaluations by the electronic brain is that the human race, contrary to popular impression, will not be extinguished in another war. Here is the electronic data, based upon the type and number of fission and fusion bombs that are likely to be used in the next war, as well as upon information concerning other weapons adapted to mass destruction:

"1. The next war would kill or disable 1,400,200,000

human beings throughout the world. (This means three out of every five persons now living.)

"Electronic estimates by countries of human dead in another war:

"Great Britain 32,430,000; France 26,172,000; Germany 49,863,000; Italy 23,497,000; Czechoslovakia 4,-958,000; Spain 29,683,000; Sweden 1,605,000; Norway 974,000; Russia 97,635,000; United States 82,582,000; Canada 8,111,000; India 62,994,000; Pakistan 17,-437,000; China 227,143,000; Burma 621,000; Japan 46,798,000; Philippines 11,222,000; Australia 2,621,000.

"2. Two thirds of the world's existing wealth would be destroyed.

"3. Destruction of cities. The electronic report is broken down by countries. It shows that in Great Britain all cities of more than 28,000 population would be totally destroyed; in France, all cities of more than 22,000; in Germany, all cities of more than 19,000; in Russia, all cities of more than 11,000; in China, all cities of more than 9,000; in the United States, all cities of more than 32,000; in Italy, all cities of more than 22,000; in Canada, all cities of more than 30,000.

"4. Life expectancy per country following another war, according to electronic analysis. In the United States of America and Europe, twenty-eight years for women; twenty-four and a half years for men. In Asia, twenty-two years for women; nineteen years for men.

"5. Value of currency after the next war. In the United States of America it will take $3,600 to buy $1 worth of goods (base year 1960); in Great Britain, 520 pounds worth one pound; in France, 800 francs worth one franc; in China, 40,000 yen worth one yen; Russia, 19,000 rubles worth one ruble.

"So much for the effects of another war as computed by the machine on the basis of actual damage in past wars and on estimates of the destructive power of the new weapons.

"Third: This phase of the electronic brain's answers concerns methods tried throughout history to preserve the peace, and the electronic brain's answer concerning ways in which the atomic war might be averted.

"1. *Peace through armament superiority.* Since 650 B.C. the nations of the world have engaged in 1,656 armaments races. These armaments races have resulted in 1,640 wars. In the sixteen occasions which did not result in war, the armaments races resulted in economic collapse.

"Building armaments is justified only as an adjunct to a larger policy. They cannot indefinitely maintain security. In fact, in the latter stages of an armaments race there was increased danger of attack because one side or the other believed it might win by a crushing attack, delivered in surprise.

"Unlimited armaments programs cripple the economy and are destructive of freedoms.

"Dispensing with armaments altogether is certain disaster. Lack of armaments under certain circumstances can be an invitation to certain aggression. From this we deduce the fact that armaments can fulfill a vital function for a limited period of time. Economically, at a certain stage, they become ruinous. Militarily, beyond a certain stage, they create a stimulus for a surprise attack. In either case, the absence or the presence of armaments cannot prevent war.

"2. *Treaties.* Treaties represent statements of intent, and seldom survive the original signers. Out of 4,711 treaties pertaining to the peace 4,697 have been broken or have failed in the past 3,200 years. The fourteen treaties that did succeed led to mutually beneficial consolidation among the nations involved.

"3. *Peace by coalition or balance-of-power.* Of the 764 such attempts which have been made, none has succeeded in fulfilling its original purpose. Forty-four coalitions were strong enough to impose their will upon weaker powers for a period greater than thirty years. Forty-two of these succumbed to internal unrest of the people. The remaining two led to binding union.

"4. *Freedom and Peace*. The final answer furnished by the brain is, of course, the most important and valuable one. Taking all the factors just stated into account and with a working knowledge of all history before it, the machine supplied a fairly short answer. As it happened, a number of human brains—without benefit of electronic impulses or automatic co-ordination—had already offered the same answer. When translated, it read as follows: 'War is not inevitable. Give the United Nations the power and the means it needs to enforce world peace through law.' "

XIV. *Don't Resign from the Human Race*

HAVE you ever wondered what you would say if you were suddenly called upon to defend the human race?

Suppose you were invited to participate in a great debate or, better still, a mock court trial called for the purpose of deciding whether the human species had justified its right to survive and whether, on the basis of its virtues and weaknesses, it was actually entitled to the gift of life. Suppose your job was that of attorney for the defense. How would you go about collecting your evidence? What witnesses would you call? What arguments would you use?

You would have the satisfaction, of course, of knowing that you represented the popular side of the argument and that the preponderance of the evidence was with you. But what do you do when you discover at the trial that your opponent has anticipated most of your arguments and, indeed, is using them against you? And what do you do when you find yourself gradually being won over by the sheer logic of his position?

Naturally, you had intended, when your turn came, to talk about the dignity and nobility of man, his capacity for great ideas, great works of art, great deeds. You had planned to describe his capacity for evolution and growth and progress. You had planned a long procession of witnesses in men who not only exemplified genius and nobility in themselves, but whose words might be used to support and dramatize your argument. You had planned to summon Aristotle as an example of the Whole Man who combined rounded, integrated knowledge with wisdom, and intelligence with conscience; one who understood the elusive but necessary balance between thought and action. And you were especially anxious to offer Aristotle's testimony that man, at his best, was the noblest creature of all. You had planned, too, to bring up Seneca as a witness, so that all might hear him say that man was a social and reasoning animal. You had planned to offer in evidence Longinus' observation that, from the moment of his birth, man had had implanted in him by nature an inextinguishable love for the noble and the good. You had planned . . .

But all these plans never materialized because your opponent, the prosecuting attorney, admitted their validity at the outset. No one could deny that individual man was capable of great deeds and words, of vast loyalty and integrity and courage. But this, he said, was not the point at issue. He then proceeded to draw a very careful sharp distinction between traits that characterized the individual and traits that characterized the species as a whole.

It was upon this distinction, he said, that he intended to build the main part of his argument. For the central question under examination concerned the entity that was the human species. There could be no doubt, he said, that countless individuals had easily justified the right to survive. However, for every symphony or work of art representing individual genius there was an instance of the collective evil of war, or of group injustice in the form of slavery, or starvation or torture. If you were to take the debits and credits on the over-all balance sheet of collective man, the final figure would not be in his favor. Nor was there in operation anywhere in the world a group conscience, as-

suming conscience to be, if not the source, at least the
filter, for determinations of right and wrong.

As soon as group conscience was mentioned, you wondered whether the prosecutor had overlooked religion.
What were the great religious traditions if not the very
means of developing the group conscience?

But the prosecutor, it appeared, had overlooked nothing.
Speaking of Christianity in particular, he said that the great
tragedy of the past two thousand years, was that man had
plucked out of it for his own use whatever seemed easiest and most convenient, ignoring the rest. He had longed
for spiritual security and he had seized upon it in Christianity. But that was only one aspect of Christianity. The
aspects of ethics in Christianity in the development of
a higher morality for himself and the group as a whole,
and the refinement of conscience—this he conveniently
ignored. Thus Christianity became not so much a new
way of life which could ennoble individual and group
behavior as a heavily subdivided and even competing series
of theological systems which man regarded most often as
offering preparation for death rather than for life. This
particular emphasis also had the effect of causing people to
regard Christianity as a convenient cleansing operation for
conscience; the burden of wrongdoing could be discarded,
thus squaring the individual with society and giving him
the conscious or subconscious satisfaction of knowing that
other such burdens might similarly be disposed of. There
grew up the phenomenon of the double standard in religion
in the believing but not practicing Christian.

Fearing it might be thought that he had been too severe
in these criticisms, the prosecutor then asked his audience
to consider honestly and frankly what the original prophets
and disciples might say about Christianity in the light of
history. Would they not repeat what has often been said:
that Christianity has yet to be tried by mankind; that the

forms it has taken are so far removed from the ideas and urgings of its Originator as to raise the question whether the continued use of the term was not actually fraudulent?

In any event, as it concerned the central question of the trial, the prosecutor said there was no evidence for claiming that religion had endowed man with the virtues which might entitle him to feel he had earned and demonstrated his right to survive. Could there be any sharper proof than was apparent in the fact that, in the name of religion itself, mass murders were carried out as one sect vied with the other in interpreting God's will and in spreading, at the point of a much-used sword, the gospel of the good, the true, and the beautiful?

Passing from religious wars to wars in general, the prosecutor asked whether Christianity or other religions had been effective in avoiding conflict in the past, or whether they were effective today in avoiding what would unquestionably be the last of the world's great wars. Here, too, the failure was dramatized by the lack of group conscience. For questions of right and wrong were absorbed and indeed obliterated by the group ego. Thus it was always the group, right or wrong. He referred to Jefferson's belief that no individual has the right to prey upon or commit aggression against the right of another individual. And yet, what happened to morality when raised to the collective level? What about the individual inside nations? What about an individual who had no choice but to join in crime and murder because society or the state arrogated to itself exemption from the moral code?

Right there, you might have thought you detected several serious weaknesses in the prosecutor's argument. Wasn't he making the mistake of oversimplifying war? Wouldn't a group be justified in going to war in a just cause? And what would the price of submission be if it failed to respond to the challenge? The American people, for example, could very easily have avoided war if they had been content to be made part of a vast dictatorial system that would have ground each individual into an evil mold. Was that what the prosecutor had in mind?

Here too, however, you quickly discovered that the prosecutor was aware of the need to qualify his argument.

Certainly, he said, a group had the right to defend itself against evil. But even in that case, the evil is represented by other human beings who, collectively, had abandoned morality. Besides, he pointed out, what really counts is the conduct and the record of humanity as a whole, rather than that of the subdivisions such as developed along national or other group lines. And it was that total appraisal of the human record that was at issue in this trial.

In the light of that appraisal, he continued, it was clear that there could be only one answer to the question under debate. Indeed, he said, what has happened might actually be called the Human Forfeit, for the right to survive was being squandered.

There seemed to be general agreement in the audience that the prosecutor had built up an impressive case, but, as people began to think and talk about it, it occurred to them that there was perhaps a basic contradiction in his argument. He had emphasized man's failure to create a group conscience. He obviously favored a world federation. Hence the possible contradiction. What point would there be in setting up a world federation only to have it crack up because man lacked the collective conscience necessary to operate it?

Apparently, the prosecutor overheard some of this comment, for when he resumed and launched into his summation, he took up this very question.

"It has not been my purpose at this trial," he began, "to present a general indictment against the human race. My purpose has been to touch upon some of those aspects of its history that bear directly on the question of the trial: has man *justified* his right to survive?

"I place special emphasis upon the word *justified* because I have deliberately avoided any opinion as to whether he will survive. That question falls more properly within the argument of the attorney for the defense.

"I have attempted at this trial to call attention to certain conspicuous failings in man's habits and conditioning and attitudes—please note that I do not say his nature—which so far have caused him great travail and anguish. I have tried to suggest that those failings have been serious in the past, but are critical now because of a fast-vanishing margin for error.

"It may have been observed that I have attempted to take an almost extra-planetary view of man. I have attempted, in general, to view him in his collective being, rather than as Americans or Russians or Englishmen or Frenchmen or Chinese or Indians or Africans and so on. It is easy but dangerous to be caught up in the passions and pressures that grow out of national differentiations. The differences between East and West that split the world today may seem deep and real to those who are involved in them. But viewed from the outside, the differences and the differentiations would seem idiotic to the point of insanity.

"To the outsider there would be only the entity of mankind. If he were to seek an objective and rational explanation for the authorized mass murder of war, or for the staggering lack of political and social justice in the world, or for the clustered misery and starvation that curse man's existence, the outsider would find it inconceivable that only one species was involved. He would be certain that some competing species was preying upon man—and perhaps vice versa.

"Might I suggest, without encroaching upon the arguments of my opponent, that some such objective view by man of himself might help him avoid his final error.

"One more point. In the course of my remarks, I have referred to the flaw in man's development which has prevented him from creating an adequate basis for existence within the group, as well as between groups. I have been concerned with his failure to invest the group with an essential moral code or conscience.

"I have also referred to his failure so far to recognize that only world government can avert the war now impending.

"There is a direct connection between the two. The immediate objective, the immediate problem is world federation. It offers the means by which the peoples of the world can build a floor over quicksand for a few years. It offers the world a chance to break away from the inevitability of war. It offers a chance to do some hard thinking and to gain the perspective and wisdom necessary for the attainment of man's indispensable and ultimate objective.

"That objective is the development and refinement of a collective conscience. In the long run, lack of it would of course destroy even (or perhaps especially) a world federation. But at least world federation might serve as the germinating agency for a collective conscience. At least it might provide the means through which a sense of community of the world's peoples can be nurtured. It could invest the term 'world citizenship' with real meaning. Perhaps a world freed of war might be able eventually to generate new habits of mutuality which could flow into that conscience.

"If you ask whether I believe the human race will actually set up a world federation and attempt to develop the conscience necessary to make it a success, I can only say I do not know. I repeat that I have concerned myself here with the unpromising record to date, and with a statement of essentials for the future. I have not ventured to predict whether those essentials would or could be recognized and met.

"For a consideration of that question, however, I now step down in favor of the attorney for the defense."

What do you do at this point? What do you say? You realize that you have been called upon to define a basis for hope. The argument you had intended to make—that the human race had *justified* its right to survive—had been fairly well demolished by the prosecutor. You had originally thought of the word "justify" as applying to the inherent virtues of individual man. But the prosecutor had used it more appropriately as applying to man's actual collective capacity, based on experience, to deal with recurring major problems.

Did this mean that there is nothing left to go on, that inevitability is sovereign, and that we might as well resign from the human race?

Certainly not. There *is* a basis for hope. For even if you agreed with everything the prosecutor said, you could properly regard his argument not as obituary but as warning. It was a stern diagnosis but it included a prescription.

Such a prescription is not beyond man's reach. Whatever his limitations may have been in the past, however great the perpetuation of error, what has to be done today is well within his capacity.

Some neurologists contend that the average individual possesses at least four or five times more brain power than he puts to use. They describe huge, unused, reserve areas of the brain as constituting vast potential reservoirs of intelligence. They see no arbitrary limits to this capacity for expansion. Only man's needs and his understanding of those needs can govern that. What, then, must be done to enable him to release and summon those vast reservoirs of intelligence that can produce the necessary vital decisions?

Perhaps the faculty of anticipation in man could do it.

Let the individual anticipate, if he can, the next war. Let him anticipate the hell of the transient survivors, however few or many. Let him anticipate his place among them—the things he would see and the things he would do.

Let him anticipate the things he would think about. Let him anticipate his disbelief that all this organized insanity should have been allowed to come to pass. Let him anticipate his certainty that all this could have been averted, for he would know then, in retrospect, what should have been done. Let him, most of all, anticipate the problem of living with his conscience.

He would think it fantastic, looking backward, that anyone anywhere should have concerned himself with anything except the drive to create a world federation in time. He would be sickened at the thought that the peoples should have allowed themselves to be persuaded by talk of difficulties and differences in the way of world federation. He would know that even if some nations declined, at least enough of the others might have rallied with America around a moral principle in pooling their sovereignty—enjoying preponderance but keeping the door open and making it clear that the purpose of the common government was a common security under justice.

This is the type of anticipatory wisdom, you might say at the trial, that is needed now. For if we have it now, there will be unlocked within us not only the essential intellectual and physical energies but the first real manifestations of collective conscience. We have nothing to lose but our adolescence.

XV. *Think of a Man*

THINK of a man.

Think of someone, living or dead, whose life has enriched your own. Think back for a moment on the name or names that have given history a forward thrust, a sense of direction, an infusion of important knowledge, an encounter with the beautiful. Names connected to great ideas or causes or deeds or works of art.

You are asked to do this because an intimate relationship, all at once, has come to exist between the lives of such men and your own. The turn of events has made you the custodian of all their works. For it is now in your power—power on a scale never before possessed by human beings—to protect and fulfill those great works and ideas or to shatter them beyond recognition or repair. There is no achievement in human experience, no record, no thing of beauty that cannot now be rescinded and all its benefits and traces swept into void. It is this that distinguishes our generation from all previous generations: we possess total authority not only over our own time but over all the ages and works of man. Earlier generations have had the power merely to affect history; ours is the power to expunge it.

We have managed somehow to unhinge the permanent. Everything that has occurred in history until now has suddenly acquired interim status. The mammoth struggles and sacrifices strung together over a period of centuries that have

180

reduced barbarism and released the human individual for creative purpose—all these are now fragile and uncertain. It is in this sense that our time has become a grand concourse for all the great causes and experiences of the race, six thousand years of them, suddenly made tentative and unresolved because of the new reach of modern man.

Think of a man. Begin in medicine. Think of the long procession of great theorists and researchers whose work has overturned the old vital statistics that condemned nine out of ten men to a lifetime under forty years. Think of the advances built on this work that now make possible great new expectations of sixty years or more for the average man in a large part of the world. But think, too, that the cures for the life-shortening diseases can now be nullified because of political diseases far more menacing to health and longevity.

More specifically, think of men such as Vesalius or Harvey who took medicine out of the dark ages by contributing so mightily to the working knowledge of the human structure in general and of the bloodstream in particular. But the principal dangers to bone and bloodstream today are far beyond the reach of the great men of medicine to combat or correct. For our age has devised a supremely efficient method of altering and damaging the balances in bone and blood. This is not difficult. Nor is it necessary to individualize the process. The blood of millions of human beings can now be altered by a political decision to throw a single switch.

If you are still thinking of warriors for better health, think of a man like Robert Koch who pried open the secrets of the bacilli, revealing powerful enemies too small to be seen by the unaided eye, and marking out for special attack the bacillus that caused tuberculosis. Or other famous microbe hunters like Van Leeuwenhoek or Pasteur or Ehrlich or Claude Bernard or Hideyo Noguchi, whose combined researches gave focus to the intricate nature of disease as well as the way to attack it. Here, too, it is important to reflect that something smaller than the bacillus or virus has become infinitely more dangerous. Neutrons released by radioactivity—visible not even to the microscope—can now surround man, piercing thick walls to get at him, shooting through every part of his being, causing his organs to function crazily or not at all. The neutrons are not hypothetical. They exist. As many as are required to twist all life out of shape can now be put to work without delay. The towering medical discoveries could be meaningless alongside this reality.

Or perhaps you have been thinking of men like Mechnikov or Cohnheim who explored the world of the cells inside the human being—an ordered world with complex but stern requirements of its own. When excessive radiation enters this world it changes it and condemns it.

If the names that come to your mind have to do with preventive medicine—names like Jenner or Lister or Semmelweiss or Agramonte or John Enders or Jonas Salk —consider that, while countless thousands have been spared smallpox or diphtheria or yellow fever or pellagra or poliomyelitis because of these medical pioneers, there are countless millions today who are totally vulnerable to the fundamental and massive threats to their health and safety represented by the combination of grandeur in science and anarchy in the world.

The names of the giants are endless. Domagk and Waksman and Fleming and Dubos; Freud and Breuer and Jackson and Jung and Brill and Chisholm; Cannon and Selye and Hench and Beck and Blalock—men of our time who have used the creative and disciplined intelligence for freeing mind and body for a longer and more purposeful existence. But, whether with respect to antibiotics or mental health or synthetic hormones or new surgical techniques, the victories in these fields can be held in escrow only until the basic health of society is assured. For when civilization itself goes insane the diagnosis and treatment of an individual are valiant but incomplete.

"Our great purpose," T. H. Huxley once wrote of science, "is the improvement of Man's estate and the widening of his knowledge. The moment a conception ceases to be useful for this purpose, away with it to the four winds; we care not what becomes of it!"

Think, then, of the men who have studied the nature of life—all the way from Aristotle and Bacon to Lamarck and Darwin and Wallace and Spencer. They tried to see man against the largest possible setting, which is to say, his natural one. And they were uninhibited in their approach. A question didn't have to have an answer, but if it was a good question it might produce three or four more questions related to it; and eventually a body of questions was formed which might add up to something.

The questions that Darwin asked had to do with the infinite variety of life but also with the basic similarities and relationships of living things. They led him to theories of change—generally change for the better, at least in terms of the need of life to adapt itself to change or die. Life was a precarious enterprise because the means of sustaining it never quite remained fixed. Different species might put in competing claims for the same means. It was natural that the species that developed sharper or more effective approaches to its changing environments would have a superior claim on survival. Natural selection, therefore, involved an upward drive or evolutionary process.

Charles Darwin's ideas represent a monumental contribution to scientific knowledge, but they have never been proved. In particular, the theory of evolution, forecast by Buffon, speculated upon by Lamarck, and developed by Darwin and Wallace, has not been proved because in six thousand years of recorded history a change from one major species into another had never been scientifically observed. But life in various forms has existed on this planet for several hundred million years and our knowledge is confined to a puny fraction of that period. As it concerns the history of man himself we have only the vaguest ideas about his age on earth, whether it covers a million years or considerably more or less.

At any rate, even without proof, Darwin's carefully assembled ideas have seemed reasonable enough to the scientific intelligence to be accepted as a working theory.

It is possible, however, that modern man may furnish proof of the Darwinian theory—in reverse. It may be entirely within the reach of man today to demonstrate the changeability of species—except that it may be devolution rather than evolution. The change may be away from higher or more selective development to less complex and cruder forms.

Though this is sheer speculation, it is possible that there can be, and perhaps already has been, retrogression of the species. Man may have gone up and down the ladder of evolution several times during his millions of years on earth. It is at least theoretically possible that he has built other civilizations as complex as our own and suffered the same inability to operate them. He may have surged far ahead in his inventiveness, but may have been deficient in creating the basis for sanity in the relations between the various groupings into which he was divided. No one can say that our generation is the first that has played with nuclear energy or that there may not have been earlier uncontrolled situations in which radioactivity brought about a whole reshuffling of species.

If limitless knowledge and applied science can create an environment in which man's basic existence is threatened, he may respond or adapt by sinking far enough in the order of intelligence so that science is beyond his reach, whether for good or evil. The tendency of nature may be to push the forms of life upward through a process of natural selection, as Darwin argued, but it may also be true that man has co-operated in this natural process only up to a point. That point in the past, as it seems to be in the present, may be a point of maximum opportunity and maximum power from which he abruptly veered away, turning his power on himself and the essence of his being.

But it is not only in medicine or the sciences that the present generation can cancel out great gains or ideas. All the fields that add up to progress for man are involved, whether one refers to the arts of man or the rights of man.

Think now of the men who proved the human being need not be condemned to the life of the drone. Here were the men who worked on the frontier of human uniqueness, expressing the need to create beauty and enabling other men to respond to it. What they did gave a necessary extra dimension to life.

One thing their works had in common, quite apart from the power to convey rhythm or harmony or a state of esthetic grace or expressive energy in general: The great paintings or songs or poems or books or edifices stand above time. They appeal to all ages; they are independent of time itself. A work of art took as long to produce as was necessary to make it a work of art. A Greek temple took a lifetime or more to build. The Taj Mahal was many years in the making. The paintings in the Dome in Milan were spaced out over a period of centuries. The massive religious sculptures and carvings at Boro Budur in Central Java were worked on for two hundred and fifty years. The creators of Kyoto and Nara, Japan, were neither pressed for time nor obsessed by fears of time when these cities devoted themselves to the cause of beauty and the permanence of beauty.

Only a second is now required to knock it all down.

Nor is the nullifying power of modern man over time and its relationship to beauty confined to the big objects that are so easily swept aside. A Giotto fresco, a window at Chartres, a poem by Aeschylus or Blake or Iqbal, a tragedy by Euripides or Shakespeare, a sermon by Donne or Tagore, an etching by Rembrandt or Turner or Hiroshige, a quartet by Mozart or Haydn, or a symphony by Beethoven—all are now equally vulnerable. It is no longer true that no force can kill a book or work of art. Obliteration can do it. Ultimate power that fulfills itself in an instant can do it. And if the force cannot find art to destroy it man can lose it by losing his own awareness of beauty. This inner loss, too, is now within his reach.

"We owe past generations," Samuel Butler once wrote, "not only for the master discoveries of music, science, literature, and art—few of which brought profit to those to whom they were revealed—but also for our organism itself, which is an inheritance gathered and garnered by those who have gone before us."

Now think of the men who were identified with great causes. Think of the men who fought to establish the most revolutionary principle in all history; namely, that the purpose of the state was to serve the cause of the individual. Think of Solon, the great law-giver of early Greece, who championed the sovereignty of the individual, beyond the reach of authority of the nation. Or Pericles, calling for equal justice toward all and arguing that public discussion, far from being a stumbling block to workable government, was an "indispensable preliminary to wise action."

Think of the men who continued and enlarged this cause, frequently at the cost of their lives. These were the leaders who believed that the act of being born carried with it a long list of natural and basic rights—political, spiritual, social. Erasmus, Milton, Harrington, Cowley, Locke, Spinoza, Montesquieu, Voltaire, Garibaldi, Mirabeau, Alfieri, Manzoni, Hume, Woolman, Penn, Fox, and the American revolutionary leaders—Franklin, Washington, Samuel Adams, John Adams, John Dickinson, Jefferson, Madison, Paine, Wilson, Hamilton, Freneau. Only a partial list but enough to serve as focus for purposeful thought about the relationship of the individual citizen to the nation. These men believed in the independence of the nation and in self-government—not as an abstraction or as an end in itself but as a specific way of protecting individual man and assuring his right to participate in the shaping of his society.

It is important to think about this concept because it has never been in greater jeopardy. What has happened is that a whole series of changes have interfered with the ability of the state to act as Jefferson or Madison or Adams felt it must act.

When a man like Jefferson thought about government the things that came to mind were not concerned with grandiose political machinery or master operational plans for the control of a nation. Each idea about government had something to do with people. Would this feature of government help a man to grow? Would that aspect of government help force errors into the open by government itself? Would this provision of government make it possible for a man to pick his own church or books or newspaper or friends? Was there any danger that government would arrogate to itself an official conscience that would seek to displace the conscience of the individual or limit its range? How could a man be fortified with rights so that overblown functionaries could not barge into his home at will just to make him squirm?

It was natural that a Jefferson would think of these things for he knew that the tendency of a state was to collect power far beyond its needs, just as it was the tendency of the men at the top to try to make a permanent acquisition of the government itself. What counted most was not the sovereignty of the state but the sovereignty of the individual. The great cause, therefore, was the cause of the individual against the state.

The cause has come a long way. If it is in danger today, however, it is not only because of the perpetual threats from dictators or ambitious men who constantly scheme to gain supremacy over the laws. The cause of individual man is in danger today because the sovereign state itself is no longer an adequate instrument for safeguarding the individual or underwriting his freedom.

It becomes necessary, then, for the individual to think not solely of the great men of the past and their legacy but of his relationship to the state in the light of new conditions.

Sovereignty will not be modified, nor a new basis for security and freedom be established, unless the individual makes it his prime concern. If enough individuals are persuaded that a new basis for human safety must be created, they can give their society a new direction and a new voice.

Men like Jefferson and Lincoln believed that every great development or change in history begins with advocacy. The change may not come about overnight; it may be stonily resisted. But there is also a natural human response to the essentials of purposeful survival. The individual who speaks to this response will be speaking the most important language on earth. He may not be able by himself to create a consensus, but he can communicate his concern. He can draw encouragement from the knowledge that the great ideas of history were originally dependent on individual advocacy and individual response.

Whether such advocacy gets through to other societies depends not solely on the thickness of the barriers surrounding those societies but on the validity of the ideas behind the advocacy and the carrying power of their genuineness. Some governments may hold back, but an idea directed to world sanity and safety cannot be muted indefinitely.

How are we to measure or test such a great idea? We measure it by its ability to fit not only *our* problem but the problems of *all*.

That problem is how to create abundance on earth and use it for greater good; how to eliminate or control the situations that lead to war, whether with respect to predatory assault or the injustice that is worse than war itself. And, if we cannot do all this, how to keep the large idea alive so that the job of the next generation can be something more inspiring than clearing away the meaningless rubble left by mighty but mediocre men.

In advocating the large idea, we can offer our pledge that we will take no measures in the cause of our own protection that will jeopardize the safety of the world community—and call upon others to do the same. We can pledge our fullest moral and material support in developing the responsible powers of the world organization so that it can truly enforce the peace.

The spirit in which such an enterprise is advocated is no less essential than the plan itself. If the spirit is one of deep affirmation and vitality, if it views the present as the rich and proper moment for the greatest forward surge in human history, then we will not invite the dangers of a purely mechanical approach to peace. Such a spirit might well be expressed in a statement of human interdependence, in which the lack of geographical or physical barriers in the world is fully recognized; in which man's right to his genetic integrity is declared; in which unity and diversity are both recognized and assured—unity in terms of the basic oneness of man, diversity in terms of his cultures or groupings or purposes; in which the natural rights of man are redefined and placed beyond the state; and in which air and earth are declared the natural assets and possessions of the world's peoples; to be utilized for the common good and to be kept free from assault or corruption by human agencies.

It is not necessary for the Soviet Union and the United States to merge or to create a political unity between them in order that sanity and safety may exist on this earth. It is necessary only that each gives up the specific right and the means to upset the vital balances which make human life on this planet possible, on conditions that the world community itself develop the workable mechanisms of law in which both can have confidence and in which both can participate for the greater good of all the earth's peoples.

If there is any other hope, then those who profess it have the obligations to define it and advocate it. Far better to have debate on world law and its alternatives than to continue a state of moral anesthesia and global anarchy which accepts any explosive situation so long as the fuse is not actually spluttering.

Let us think, then, about ourselves. If our purposes are frail, if the value we attach to idea of progress is small, if our concern for the next generation is uninspiring, then we can bow low before the difficulty, stay as we are, and accept the consequences of drift. But if we have some feeling for the gift of life and the uniqueness of life, if we have confidence in freedom, growth, and the miracle of vital change, then difficulty loses its power to intimidate.

No greater fallacy exists in the modern world than that the individual in a free society is helpless. If anything, he exercises his power without being aware of it. Vast sums are spent to find out what he thinks or is likely to think. No major move can be made without him.

The question for the individual is not whether he possesses any power but how to use the power he possesses. He will receive information if he demands it. He can appraise information if he will give time to it. He can think, he can talk, he can write, he can associate, he can make his opinions known. He need not wait to be asked for his views. He can free himself from the daily trivia that soak up his time and energies and he can apply himself to what is important. Nor need he fear that this is an academic or futile undertaking. The act of informed dedication is a power by itself.

As the individual thinks about the power that is his—the power to think and act in behalf of history's great works and ideas of which he is now custodian—he may find that information and thought are not enough. It is one thing to know a fact, another to interpret it and relate it to other facts with order and balance.

He can consult other individuals; he can also consult history. He can tap the experience of the race. He can find out something about the great causes he is now asked to protect. And he can think about the great spiritual leaders in human history and ask himself what their response would be to the forces of man that now jeopardize the estate of man. He can think about the prophets of the Old Testament and their emphasis on respect for the universal design and their insistence on justice. He can think about the purity, simplicity, and grandeur of the morals and ideals and teachings of Jesus, and the power of dedication of the Apostles. He can think about the reforming zeal and desire for spiritual emancipation of Mohammed. About the Deities of the Veddas, with their seamless and poetic continuity between life and the universe. About Buddha's concern for the individual in stress and suffering and the higher reality of which he is part and which knits him together. About Bahaullah and his effort to provide a basis for spiritual and social unity among all men. About the ethics and restraint and service to humanity of Confucius.

It should not be difficult for the individual to determine

what the spiritual leaders would say in the present situation. They would say that it is not enough for man to profess oneness with other men; he must act it out. Not enough to wear the garment of religious identification; he must accept its ethical and moral obligations and glory. Not enough to lay claim to personal sacredness; he must bind himself to it through respect for it and sensitivity to it. Not enough to boast of the gift of a rational intelligence; he must nurture it, work it, apply it, defend it. Not enough to prate about justice; he must create a basis for it in the world itself.

The individual who believes he is powerless to affect history marks the beginning of the failure that multiplies itself until it finally takes the form of men who smash at the very conditions in nature that make life possible. And the evil will continue until men see their connections to each other and to the large body or community of which each is a part.

XVI. *An Exciting Time To Be Alive*

IF you had the entire range of history spread out before you, what period would you choose in which to live? What age of man would you consider most satisfying or exciting?

The late Irwin Edman once suggested that the end of the nineteenth century and the first decade of the twentieth century was an ideal period for a reasonable man; and Professor Edman placed a high value indeed on reasonable men. Professor Edman liked the spaciousness and graciousness of the period. Democratic government existed throughout most of Western civilization. People were not being pushed around in large numbers by dictators. Machines at that time were still things that human beings could control. A man had time to think and read. Discussion was one of the lively arts. The life of the mind really came to something. And, most important of all, it seemed to the reasonable men of the period that the mutual mass slaughter that went by the name of war was a thing of the long ago.

The late Carl Becker, one of the most sensitive and worldly of American historians, had a proper appreciation of the period from 1880 to 1910, but his imagination was captured by the men and the events of a century earlier. What happened in Europe and America through most of the eighteenth century, especially during the latter half, was to him as glorious and rich an age as the world had ever known. For it was in that period that human intelligence made its great conquests—not conquests in invention but in human affairs. Ideas about the natural rights of man were being connected up to free will. People were discovering that they could fashion their own destiny and that the state could exist as the principal means of serving the individual. It was an Age of Reason; it was also an Age of Action. Professor Becker liked to call it the "heavenly city of the eighteenth-century philosophers" because it really seemed at the time that thoughtfulness, decency, and nobility of spirit would be dominant in the affairs of man.

Historians on ancient Greece would be certain to put in a claim for the Golden Age in the fifth century B.C. Men like Gilbert Murray or A. E. Zimmern or F. M. Cornford or C. A. Robinson, Jr. would probably call attention to the fact that never before or since has there been such a concentration of the creative intelligence at work as existed in Athens at its zenith. They would point to the Periclean Era as something of an adventure in human awareness. The probing, searching, artistic spirit was at work. It was an age thirsty for knowledge and achievement. The scientific spirit and method came alive, whether with respect to government, mathematics, geometry, astronomy, physics, or logic itself. Equally significant was the sense of beauty and the attention to beauty in the art and architecture and in the lives of the people.

An historian and speculative thinker such as H. G. Wells would probably have said that we ought to enlarge our view. Judging from his books, he might have nominated the T'ang Dynasty in China, seventh to ninth centuries A.D. He might have pointed to the Chinese art of living, to the freedom men enjoyed from the need to possess things, to the stability of individual life, to the advanced development of architecture and painting and poetry, and the existence of printing long before the West thought of it. Or Wells, like Emerson and Ruskin, might have held up any one of a half dozen or more periods in the history of India as candidates for the most satisfying time to be alive. In particular the Gupta Age during the fourth and fifth centuries A.D. This was the age of the Golden Peace when India, secure from invasion and internal conflict, ascended the heights. Government was enlightened; the land was good and rich; there were monumental achievements in science, music, literature, painting.

All these are noble and inspiring periods of human history. As for ourselves, we choose the present. The danger to human mind and flesh may never have been greater. The means for cheapening life and brutalizing it may never have been so highly developed, so easy to use. There may never have been so many distractions and trivia to assault the mind, to pull it in so many petty directions. Nor has there ever been an age in which so many men gave so little thought to the vital things that concerned their destiny.

Despite it all, despite the hydrogen bombs and the intercontinental ballistic missiles and the fumbling of the statesmen while the fuses of nuclear war are spluttering, we would still choose the present. Just think of what we win if we win. No other age in history has had the same potential. About no earlier period in history could it be said that the earth could be made sufficient for the needs of all its people. The conquest of disease and poverty is clearly within reach. Hunger and thirst can be made technologically obsolete; the control of solar energy for utilizing photosynthesis is a specific and attainable prospect. Man has the potential sources of energy that can give him time to fulfill himself and develop his creative resources on a scale and with an intensity that have never before been possible.

From 1945 to 1960, the human species has had to withstand and comprehend greater and more fundamental changes than have been recorded in all the histories since man first began to record his histories. In fifteen years, change has overtaken almost the entire body of science and systematic knowledge. The one event represented by the liberation of atomic energy may have greater significance than any previous utilization of the scientific intelligence of man. The conquest of earth gravity, as represented by the man-made satellite, may have an even more profound effect on philosophy than upon physics. A sudden new perspective bursts upon the mind. The human brain now begins to perceive, however dimly, the meaning of a universe in which the earth and, indeed, the solar system may occupy a position in relationship to the whole no larger than the atom itself is to this planet.

Nothing has been more difficult in the evolution of thought than for man to depart from his view of himself as central in the universe. But now we have to begin to live with the idea that life, life with intelligence, may exist on millions or billions of planets and may even, in many cases, be far superior to our own. And the successful exploration of space is an even more realistic prospect than was the exploration of the new world at the end of the fifteenth century.

Meanwhile, the entire human grouping exists in an arena of change. Man is developing new abilities, new philosophies, new vistas; he can also develop new and exciting allegiances and loyalties. These new allegiances need not replace the existing ones; in fact, they can give them added meaning. Loyalty to a human commonwealth need not replace or supersede loyalty to the nation; it becomes a logical extension, in the same way that loyalty to the nation was an extension of loyalty to a region or tribe.

The uniqueness of the human mind is precisely that it is potentially capable not only of recognizing the fact of change but of devising the means for meeting it.

Consider man's genius at conversion, which is one specific aspect of the challenge of change.

Man can convert the face of nature into a countenance congenial to human life. He can convert sand, stone, and water into gleaming and wondrous towers. He can convert fluids into fabrics. He can convert the incisible atom into an infinity of power. He can convert the rush of water into the whirling fantasy of the dynamo and thence into the magic impulses that banish darkness or turn wheels or carry images and voices over empty space. He can even convert air, agitated by the spin of a blade or the thrust of a jet, into the lifting power that enables him to rise from the earth and fly over the mountains and the seas.

What man most needs now is to apply his conversion skills to those things that are essential for his survival. He needs to convert facts into logic, free will into purpose, conscience into decision. He needs to convert historical experience into a design for a sane world. He needs to convert the vast processes of education into those ideas that can make this globe safe for the human diversity. And he will have to learn more than he knows now about converting the individual morality into a group ethic.

Our failure to develop these conversion skills has converted us into paupers. The plenty produced by our scientific and physical skills has not relieved the poverty of our purposes. The only thing greater than our power is our insecurity. All our resources and all our wealth are not enough to protect us against the effects of irrational ideas and acts on the world stage. It makes little difference how magnificent are our new buildings or how impressive are our private kingdoms. If no answer is found to war, all men will die poor.

Man, finally, needs to convert his fears about peace into muscular thoughts about his capacities.

One fear about peace, seldom expressed but nonetheless real, is that the economy would collapse if the billions of dollars now going into military expenditures were to be cut off.

No one wants war. Yet there is a feeling that we need the threat of war if we are to avert a depression. A vital part of the nation's economy has been tied to military production for so long that there is fear that it has become part of the economic metabolism.

This fear is tied to the assumption that once the wheels of the factories stop turning and the circulating power of the defense billions are cut off, there will be nothing to take its place.

This assumption is incorrect.

In economic terms, the advantage of high military spending is not confined to the fact that it pumps considerable additional capital into the national bloodstream. It bypasses the main problem of a free economy.

The recurrent problem of a free economy is that production generally increases faster than consumption. The point of breakdown usually occurs in marketing and distribution. A military economy doesn't have to contend with this problem. The market is assured. The goods are presold. There may be rapid obsolescence but this doesn't affect either the price of the product or the point of sale. Military spending doesn't have to account for a substantial fraction of the economy in order to have a substantial impact. Even if it represents only a fourth of the gross national product, it can mean the difference between a sluggish economy and a prosperous one.

There are also dangers.

The greatest of these is that many people will want to hold on to the arms race even though a genuine opportunity may present itself for arms elimination under genuine world control. And human experience has yet to furnish an example of a major arms race that did not end in war.

If the fear of depression is greater than the fear of war, there will be war.

A sane foreign policy, therefore, begins with the declaration that we would rather have the worst depression the world has ever known than increase the risk of nuclear war.

But there need be neither nuclear war nor depression. It is possible to have peace without economic collapse. Once the United Nations is strong enough to provide a genuine basis for security and once nuclear weapons can be brought under control, the stage will be set for the effective conversion of the national economy to peace.

As production for war is eliminated, production for peace can be worked into the national economy. Here are some of the vital elements that could both supply the vital fraction required by the domestic economy and contribute powerfully to the world's needs:

1. Manufacture of 100,000,000 prefabricated three-room homes, for shipment to and assembly in those countries, principally in Asia and Africa, in which homelessness is a major problem.

2. Construction of community development projects for relocating the major refugee groups in the world, be they Arab, Pakistani, Indian, or whatever, so long as the necessary land is contributed by the respective governments.

3. Large-scale hydroelectric power projects, irrigations projects, road-building projects, health-center and hospital-building projects in other countries on the basis of long-term credits.

4. The use of agricultural surpluses to help meet the

stark fact of hunger that now affects at least one-third of the world's peoples.

One of the principal arguments in favor of such a program, if related to the work of the United Nations, is that it defines a moral standard. The entire world has been spending approximately 200 billion dollars each year for war preparations; such a sum, if made available to the special health, education, and economic agencies of the United Nations, could change the face of history.

Such, at least, is the prospect. The prospect may be bright but it is not easy. Even so, it is not beyond reach. Whether it will be done depends less on physical problems and resources than it does on the moral imagination.

There is no need to take the fatalistic view and say it is too late, that man cannot possibly develop the comprehension necessary to deal with change in the modern world, that he will require many centuries before his conversion skills can be developed as they now need to be developed in the cause of human survival.

We can take the large view of man. We can say that the great responses already exist inside him and that these responses need only to be invoked to become manifest. We can say that man is infinitely malleable, infinitely perfectable, infinitely capacious, and that it is a privilege to speak to these towering possibilities.

We need not be prisoners of drift. There is no law in history that says that men cannot reverse their direction and drive boldly forward for the things that are good and that can be theirs. Nothing is more characteristic of history than the suddenness of its shifts when enough men become aware of a large purpose. The development of an awareness of that purpose is the golden opportunity for all those who attach importance to human life and who are willing now to accept the claim upon us of the generations to come. It's an exciting time to be alive.

XVII. *First Things First*

IN THE course of history, four great struggles have dominated human imagination and purpose.

The first has been for safety against the elements and for subsistence.

The second has been for freedom and growth.

The third has been for development and distinction.

The fourth has been for safety of man against war.

Great gains have been recorded in the first three of these struggles.

The battle against heat, cold, water, sand, and ice is no longer a dominant preoccupation of man as a whole. Theoretically it is at least now possible to develop the world's resources to the point where the human population will have enough to eat. Theoretically, too, it is at least now possible to develop enough energy to bring the central benefits of an industrial civilization to most of the world's peoples.

The battle for freedom has not yet been won; it may never be won. But at least the foundations of freedom have been laid and the principles established for many millions of the earth's population. In the total perspective of human experience, freedom still has the status of an experiment; but it has been a magnificent experiment, successful in enough instances to demonstrate the creative genius of a principled society. The cause of freedom, however, is jeopardized midway through the twentieth century not only by those who are working for authoritarianism of one color or another but by a breakdown in human organization. For freedom cannot exist without law, just as law cannot exist without government; and the world as a whole today is still in a primitive, pregovernment form.

The struggle for distinction is concerned primarily with education. Most of the world's peoples are still strangers to the written word; the entire process of formal education is known only to a minority. The development of the human potential has so far been minimal—whether with respect to the individual or humankind as a whole. Yet no field of human need can be more effectively met than this. There is no insuperable problem in the way of educating men and developing their innate resources.

The fourth struggle—for safety of man against war—has been the only one of man's struggles in which he has known mounting defeat.

In no other field of human enterprise or aspiration has progress been as essential as in this; in no other field has the absence of progress been more marked or costly. The failure has grown from the earliest times, when the individual was totally without the protection of society or group, to the point when human society is completely vulnerable and unprotected.

There has never been any great difficulty in killing a man. Given the intent, the means were relatively simple. But society always did its best to interpose itself between the killer and the intended victim. It would outlaw concealed weapons; it would establish drastic punishments as deterrents; it would direct many of its efforts and facilities toward safeguarding a man against the predatoriness, the rapacity, and violence of his neighbors. Religions would lend their full force to the moral injunctions against violence.

These protections are now virtually meaningless alongside the utter ease with which society itself can put an end to life. None of its skills, indeed, have been more highly developed than this. To be able to put death into the air without changing the odor or the texture of the air; to be able to create invisible bullets that pierce skin and bone and rip open human chromosomes and genes; to be able to devise lethal droplets, any one of which can terminate life in brief contact with the human skin; to be able to tamper with the precarious balances through which nature serves all life; to be able to twist a man's character all out of shape and control his thoughts—these skills are all now claimed by human intelligence in the name of national security.

Man today is not safe in the presence of man. The old cannibalism has given way to anonymous action in which the killer and the killed do not know each other, and in which, indeed, the very fact of mass death has the effect of making the killing less reprehensible than the death of a single man.

In short, man has evolved in every respect except his ability to protect himself against human intelligence. His knowledge is vast but does not embrace the workings of peace. Because he attaches importance to a rounded view of life he studies history, philosophy, religions, languages, literature, art, architecture, political science. Because he is concerned about his well-being he studies anthropology, biology, medicine, psychology, sanitation. Because he is interested in technical progress he studies chemistry, physics, engineering, mathematics, sanitation. But he has yet to make peace basic in his education. The most important subject in this world is hardly taught at all. The basic principles involved in creating a situation of safety, the effective limits of national sovereignty; the fundamental elements that must go into the making of world law—unless these are pursued and understood, nothing else he knows will do him any good. But such knowledge is not now a fixed and essential part of the educational goals he has set for himself.

All men—whether they go by the name of Americans or Russians or Chinese or British or Malayans or Indians or Africans—have obligations to one another that transcend their obligations to their sovereign societies.

For the conflicts that involve twentieth-century man are not solely ideological or political. They are personal, historic, transcendent. They involve his relationship to others all the way from the immediate community that surrounds him to the human commonwealth as a whole.

These conflicts can be resolved in terms of first principles:

If there is a conflict between the security of the sovereign state and the security of the human commonwealth, the human commonwealth comes first.

If there is a conflict between the well-being of the nation and the well-being of mankind, the well-being of mankind comes first.

If there is a conflict between the needs of this generation and the needs of all the later generations, the needs of the later generations come first.

If there is a conflict between the rights of the state and the rights of man, the rights of man come first. The state justifies its existence only as it serves and safeguards the rights of man.

If there is a conflict between public edict and private conscience, private conscience comes first.

If there is a conflict between the easy drift of prosperity and the ordeal of peace, the ordeal of peace comes first.

With these first principles in operation, the people can create a mandate for government. Such a mandate would enable the nation to put first things first. The nation can declare that, even in its self-defense, it will not engage in a war that would destroy the rest of the world. Neither will it hesitate to declare that it would rather die than be the first to use chemical, biological, or nuclear weapons on human beings.

It could declare that it considers it a privilege to commit and dedicate everything it has—its resources, energy, knowledge, and moral imagination—to the making of a genuine peace under justice and law.

All things are possible if we do not crave the distinction of being the last generation of men on earth.

XVIII. *Checklist of Enemies*

The enemy is not solely the unfettered sovereign national state, violating the natural rights of man and jeopardizing his natural environment.

Nor is the enemy solely an atomic muscled totalitarian power with a world ideology.

The enemy is many people. He is a man whose only concern about the world is that it stay in one piece during his own lifetime. He is invariably up to his hips in success and regards his good fortune not as a challenge to get close to the real problems of the age but as proof of the correctness of everything he does. Nothing to him is less important than the shape of things to come or the needs of the next generation. Talk of the legacy of the past or of human destiny leaves him cold. Historically, he is the disconnected man. Hence, when he thinks about the world at all, it is usually in terms of his hope that the atomic fireworks can be postponed for fifteen or twenty years. He is an enemy because he is detached from the kind of concern for the rights of unborn legions that will enable the world itself to become connected and whole.

The enemy is a man who not only believes in his own helplessness but actually worships it. His main article of faith is that there are mammoth forces at work which the individual cannot possibly comprehend, much less alter or direct. And so he expends vast energies in attempting to convince other people that there is nothing they can do. He is an enemy because of the proximity of helplessness to hopelessness.

The enemy is a man who has a total willingness to delegate his worries about the world to officialdom. He assumes that only the people in authority are in a position to know and act. He believes that if vital information essential to the making of public decisions is withheld, it can only be for a good reason. If a problem is wholly or partially scientific in nature, he will ask no questions even though the consequences of the problem are political or social. He is an enemy because government, by its very nature, is unable to deal effectively today with matters concerned with human survival. It is now necessary to tame the national sovereignties and create a design of the whole. If this is to be done, it can be done not by the national sovereignties themselves but by insistent acts of the public will.

The enemy is any man in government, high or low, who keeps waiting for a public mandate before he can develop big ideas of his own, but who does little or nothing to bring about such a mandate. Along with this goes an obsessive fear of criticism. To such a man, the worst thing in the world that can happen is to be accused of not being tough-minded in the nation's dealings with other governments. He can take in his stride, however, the accusation that he is doing something that may result in grave injury to the human race. He lives entirely on the plane of plot-and-counter-plot, where the dominant reality is represented by scoring points on a day-by-day basis. He figures security largely in terms of statistics—generally in terms of the kind of force that can be put to work in a showdown situation—rather than in terms of the confidence and good will a nation may enjoy among its neighbors in the world. He is an enemy because he sees no connection between his own authority and the need to act in behalf of the human community.

The enemy is any man in the pulpit who by his words

*and acts encourages his congregation to believe that the
main purpose of the church or the synagogue is to provide
social respectability for its members. He talks about the
sacredness of life but he never relates that concept to the
real and specific threats that exist today to such sacredness.
He identifies himself as a man of God but feels no urge to
speak out against a situation in which the nature of man is
likely to be altered and cheapened, the genetic integrity of
man punctured, and distant generations condemned to a
lower species. He is a dispenser of balm rather than an
awakener of conscience. He is preoccupied with the need to
provide personal peace of mind rather than to create a
blazing sense of restlessness to set things right. He is an
enemy because the crisis today is as much a spiritual crisis
as it is a political one.*

*At a time when everything we are and everything we
have are in jeopardy, it may help to know the faces of the
enemy.*